The Roots of American Culture

Books by Constance Rourke

TRUMPETS OF JUBILEE (1927)

TROUPERS OF THE GOLD COAST (1928)

AMERICAN HUMOR (1931)

DAVY CROCKETT (1934)

AUDUBON (1936)

CHARLES SHEELER (1938)

THE ROOTS OF AMERICAN CULTURE (1942)

The Roots of American Culture

and Other Essays

BY CONSTANCE ROURKE

EDITED, WITH A PREFACE,
BY VAN WYCK BROOKS

NEW YORK
HARCOURT, BRACE AND COMPANY

BL
BRD

Preface

WHEN Constance Rourke died in 1941, she had gone far in a work that would have given her a unique position among the American writers of her day. This work, a History of American Culture, was to have filled three volumes, presenting a point of view that was wholly her own. It was to have been the expression of thirty years of exploration during which she had published a series of preliminary volumes. These six books were her *Audubon* and *Davy Crockett,* a study of the artist Charles Sheeler, *Trumpets of Jubilee, Troupers of the Gold Coast* and, finest of all, the well-known *American Humor.* With their charming qualities of style and their freshness of feeling, these books were exceptionally interesting in their own right, and it was only in retrospect that one could see how fully they were outgrowths of a single conception and a governing idea. But it was this idea, which her history would have disclosed at length, that makes the work of Constance Rourke important, and, seen in the light of her final studies, it adds to the importance of all her apparently sporadic earlier achievements.

What this idea was can best be seen and understood in

relation to a more general movement of thought. Constance Rourke began to write at a moment when the American mind was intensely concerned with itself, past, present and future, a moment of self-recognition that was marked by a number of writers who were bent on exploring the culture and resources of the country. Born at Cleveland in 1885, a graduate of Vassar in 1907, a student at the Sorbonne and for several years an instructor at Vassar, Constance Rourke shared in this movement of thought. With her deep roots in the Middle West, she pondered over the statement, so frequently made by other critics, that America had no esthetic tradition of its own. Was it true, she asked herself, that we had failed to produce a culture in which the arts could flourish? If this was true, it was serious, it was ominous indeed, for no art had ever reached a point where it could speak a world-language without an inheritance of local expression behind it. Occasional peaks of achievement did not alter this rule. As Constance Rourke said later in her study of Charles Sheeler, "Art has always taken on a special native fibre before it assumes the greater breadth;" and therefore an American esthetic tradition was a desideratum that was not to be lightly given away. It was so fundamental that it was not to be surrendered unless there were positive proofs that it did not exist. And how far had American criticism explored this subject? As for the tradition itself, if this could be shown to exist it might make

all the difference for the future of our art and all the difference, meanwhile, for the creative worker. What would
not our artists gain in maturity and confidence if they felt
that they were working "in a natural sequence"?

It was in some such terms as these that Constance
Rourke posed her problem, well knowing that if she could
solve it successfully and fully the consequences might be
important for American art. Meanwhile, she had been
drawn to the theories of Herder, of which Whitman had
seen the implications, theories that had been distorted in
the interests of antiquarianism but never, as she felt, truly
explored. According to Herder, the folk-forms were essential in any communal group, they were the texture of the
communal experience and expression, and the fine arts
sprang out of the folk-arts and one had to look to these
in order to find the source of any culture. Here Constance
Rourke found herself challenged at the outset. That
America had no folk-art was the general opinion: it was
all but universally believed that we had no folk-expression
aside from vestigial remains of European culture. Constance Rourke was not deterred by this belief, and she
felt that our dominant conception of culture was wrong.
Culture, according to this idea, was something to be imposed from without by a process known as the "transit of
civilization." It was John Fiske who used this phrase, and
it was Fiske's conception that "carriers" were to bring us
piecemeal the culture of Europe; and it was assumed that

if we dipped deeply enough into the main streams of European culture we might ultimately hope to witness their rise in this country. In the meantime, we were the victims of a "cultural lag;" and Constance Rourke opposed this theory because it led us to disregard the ways in which every culture has actually developed. It goes without saying that she did not wish to isolate us from these main streams of European culture. She welcomed them all, but that was another matter. She merely said that the question was not whether we might "catch up" with Europe, the question was one of finding a center of our own, and the center of every culture has always existed within the social organism of the country itself. Was it true, then, to return to Herder, that we really had no folk-forms? Was it not rather the case that we had a long folk-life behind us which had found inevitable expression in forms of its own? Had not the critics ignored the creative forces that have always existed in this country? And could these not be shown to constitute an esthetic tradition?

To prove the existence of this tradition, to reveal it in manifold ways was Constance Rourke's purpose in all her writings. She felt that if she could assemble materials enough, the tradition would declare itself through them, and she wished to make our natural inheritance accessible in order that it might nourish the workers of the future, placing them in possession of characteristic native forms

which they might use to advantage as points of departure.
Her work was thus mainly exploratory, and she threw herself into it with a zest that took her into every corner of
the country. She studied American architecture, the early
American theater, early American music, the American
novel, Negro folklore, the old Shaker colonies, the religious life of the country, its painting and its crafts. She
was one of the organizers of the national folk-festivals at
St. Louis. For a year she was editor of the Index of American Design, that remarkable assemblage of the folk-art of
the country, its wood-carving, textiles, embroideries, pot-
tery and glass. One of her friends has described a journey
through New England when she was looking especially
for old wall-paintings, of which she found fine specimens
at Newburyport and Lyme, and she was deeply interested
in the crafts of the Pennsylvania Germans. Their architectural forms proved to her that "the classic has nothing to
do with grandeur." But the culture of these regions was
already sufficiently well known and her most striking discoveries were made in the West, in the old frontier regions where it had been so generally thought that nothing
of the nature of art had ever existed. This was Constance
Rourke's own country, and the past of the frontier was in
her bones. One of her great-grandfathers, George Mayfield, had been a friend of David Crockett, and because
of his knowledge of the Tennessee Indians he had acted
as Jackson's interpreter in the war with the Creeks. This

George Mayfield was one of the white children who had
been stolen by the Creeks. He had been brought up by
them and never felt at ease with the whites when he was
returned to his people at his coming of age, and he often
lived with the tribe for months at a time. George Mayfield was one of the many frontiersmen who were drawn
to Indian life, and a deep feeling for the frontier was bred
in Constance Rourke and later found expression in several
of her books. These were the regions where Timothy
Flint, in the eighteen-thirties and forties, had confidently
looked for heroic expression; and there she made her own
most original discoveries in the field of the folk-arts as
well as of legend.

Meanwhile, her interest was never antiquarian, and she
never lost sight of her purpose in studying these arts.
With her sympathetic gift for drawing out all sorts of
people, she talked with old-timers who remembered this
work in the making, and she was astonished by the richness of our native design, our native skills developed on
native ground. In the general haste of our life and its
continual migrations, many of the evidences of these arts
were lost. Countless traces of our early culture were
blotted out, for the mere force of migration had destroyed
small tangible things and always tended to eliminate
them. Then there had been the destructive force of fire.
There had been holocausts of all these objects in the burning of cabins, stockades and wooden towns. But enough

had remained or were still to be found, and they showed the abundant existence of creative forces to which critics had paid small attention. Constance Rourke had assembled proofs of a rich creative life in our past, and she had found indications in it of distinctive native American elements. Derived as it may have been from Europe, our early culture diverged from Europe in accordance with our native experience and needs.

Her history would have attempted to show how far this was true, and some of the papers that follow already show it. She points out, for instance, how colonial Annapolis, which was sometimes called the American Bath, differed in its easy spaciousness from the English Bath. She shows how American Calvinism diverged from English Calvinism and formed a wholly new cultural pattern, how all our original patterns of thought and feeling were gradually "pulled into new dimensional forms." It was so in our early theater, in our early music. The motivating ideas from Europe were shaped to our own distinctive ends, and Constance Rourke shows how the fumblings of our nascent culture sprang from a life and experience that were peculiar to the country. There was no phase of American culture that she had not planned to include in this monumental survey, and it is more than regrettable that she was unable to finish the very ambitious task she had set for herself. I have been able to salvage only a few fragments from the great mass of her half-written

manuscripts and notes, but these are enough to show, I
think, how important the work would have been for artists and writers and students of American culture. As they
stand, these fragments, side by side with her other books,
reveal the rich stores of tradition that lie behind us, the
many streams of native character and feeling from which
the Americans of the future will be able to draw.

VAN WYCK BROOKS

Contents

Acknowledgment is made to the editors of *Magazine of Art* and *The Nation* for permission to reprint, respectively, "American Art: A Possible Future" and "Voltaire Combe."

The Roots of American Culture

THE ARTS have always traveled westward, and there is no doubt of their flourishing hereafter on our side of the Atlantic," wrote Benjamin Franklin to the struggling young artist Charles Willson Peale soon after the Revolution.

The prophecy was spacious, Franklin's use of the indefinite "hereafter" was significant. At another time he spoke on this subject with his customary precision. "All things have their season, and with young countries as with young men, you must curb their fancy to strengthen their judgment. . . . To America, one schoolmaster is worth a dozen poets, and the invention of a machine or the improvement of an implement is of more importance than a masterpiece of Raphael. . . . Nothing is good or beautiful but in the measure that it is useful: yet all things have a utility under particular circumstances. Thus poetry, painting, music (and the stage as their embodiment) are all necessary and proper gratifications of a refined state of society but objectionable at an earlier period, since their cultivation would make a taste for their enjoyment precede its means."

At about the same time Washington declared "that

only arts of a practical nature would for a time be esteemed," adding that it was easy to perceive the causes which have combined to render the genius of this country scientific rather than imaginative. And in this respect surely America has furnished her quota. Franklin, Rittenhouse, and Rush are no mean names.

John Adams often trenched upon these questions, at times with a touch of personal ambition: "I wish I had leisure and tranquillity to amuse myself with those elegant and ingenious arts of painting, sculpture, architecture, and music. A taste for all of them is an agreeable accomplishment." Alas! he could never take time, he explained, to write with brevity, much less to polish his periods in such a manner as to give them the aspect of literature. He argued that the arts in all ways were luxuries and so in the nature of things a democracy would fail to provide patrons for them. Its people were too poor, too greatly concerned with the business of making a living. Still further, they would lack taste, and with homely detail he considered this problem as it would affect the artist. "Why is it," he asked, that "artists . . . renounce their pleasures, neglect their exercise, and destroy their health—for what? . . . Their universal object and idol is . . . *reputation*. It is the notoriety, the celebration, which constitute the charm that is to compensate for the loss of appetite and sleep, and sometimes of riches and honors. . . . Men of letters must have a great deal of praise." In a democracy this "celebration" would not occur. "The

people" would bestow "their applauses and adorations
. . . too often . . . on artifices and tricks." Finally, he
remarked with bitterness, they would expect to receive
the arts "gratis."

Then Adams condemned the arts altogether, anticipating by almost a century, as had Franklin, an opinion
of Mark Twain's Connecticut Yankee about the art of
Raphael: "I would not give sixpence for a picture of
Raphael or a statue of Phidias." He went on with heat,
"The age of painting has not yet arrived in this country,
and I hope it will not arrive very soon." And with one of
his whirlwinds of wordy logic Adams argued that the arts
sprang from luxury, that riches created despotisms, that
the arts had been prostituted to the service of despotism
and superstition from the dawn of history, and so should
be avoided in the young nation.

As a member of a committee for the House in Massachusetts, Adams had, in 1770, drawn up a plan for the
encouragement of agriculture, commerce and the arts;
and a few years later he had formulated resolutions with
the same objectives for the Continental Congress. But it
is clear from the contexts that he was using "arts" in accordance with eighteenth-century practice to include invention, artisanship, or even science, with an emphasis
upon high excellence.[1] Washington in the first draft of his

---

[1] Jefferson in his *Notes on Virginia* applied the word in the same way,
speaking of Rittenhouse: "As an artist he has exhibited as great a proof
of mechanical genius as the world has ever produced. He has not indeed
made a world; but he has by imitation approached nearer its maker

farewell to arms included a similar passage expressing his conviction that the federal government should promote literature and the arts, and later regretted that Hamilton had persuaded him to omit this passage; but Washington also seems to have had in mind mainly the practical arts, just as by literature he certainly meant what Adams had meant in phrasing the ratification of a new charter for Harvard College in these years. Adams spoke of the encouragement of literature as a noble purpose for the college, but, as the terms indicate, he was considering literature that had the practical aims of elevation or instruction, such as writings on religion, philosophy and government. Even as to the drama, which he loved as dearly as music, Washington's judgment was practical; he considered the drama "a chief refiner." It would, he said, "advance the interest of private and political virtue . . . and have a tendency to polish the manners and habits of society." But he feared the country was too poor to afford this luxury.

No one of these statesmen expected the emergence of a professional class whose occupation was the arts. "We have no distinct class of *literati* in this country," wrote Jefferson to John Waldo in 1813. "Every man is engaged in some industrious pursuit." Twelve years later, almost at the end of his life, he wrote to a correspondent in England, "Literature is not yet a distinct profession with us.

than any man who has lived from creation to this day." Jefferson referred to Rittenhouse's model of the planetary system called the orrery.

Now and then a strong mind arises, and at its intervals of leisure from business emits a flash of light. But the first object of young societies is bread and covering."

2

Yet Jefferson was by no means discouraged as to the growth of the arts in America, "the child of yesterday." His own architectural studies in France, which he was to use for the service of Virginia and the nation, had begun in 1779. Nor was he indifferent to the possible contribution of the man of letters to our society; on the contrary, in his defense of his appointment of Freneau as a translating clerk in 1792 he formulated a far-reaching principle. Hamilton had denounced the appointment with the charge that Jefferson had made it because of Freneau's support in the partisan *National Gazette*. Jefferson wrote to Washington in passionate protest: "But you, sir, who have received from me recommendations of a Rittenhouse, Barlow, and Paine, will believe that talents and science are sufficient motives with me in appointments to which they are fitted, and that Freneau, as a man of genius, might thus find a preference in my eye to be a translating clerk. . . . I hold it to be one of the distinguishing excellences of elective over hereditary successions that the talents which nature has provided in sufficient proportion should be selected for the government of their affairs."

As to the high quality of Freneau's poetic gifts, Jefferson might have been mistaken, but there was no question as to the breadth of his underlying philosophy. What he had in mind lay outside the familiar habit of literary subsidy or patronage. Freneau, Barlow, Paine and Rittenhouse had not been given posts to provide them with stipends by means of which they might follow their private pursuits in science or literature in a possible margin of time. They had been included within the government because Jefferson believed their talents would be more serviceable there. He hoped that genius would become useful in the affairs of the republic. This concept was full of vitality, pushing to its full extreme the view of the other statesmen that to have a valid place in the new nation the arts must be related to the common life.

As to the character of the practical arts, Jefferson offered certain broad suggestions when he explained the purposes he had kept in mind in writing that supreme example of practical letters, the Declaration of Independence. For one thing, such writings need not be original in thought or manner. Jefferson sought "not to find out new principles, or new arguments, never before thought of, not merely to say things which had never been said before; but to place before mankind the common sense of the subject in terms so plain and firm as to command their assent. . . . Neither aiming at originality of principle or sentiment, nor yet copied from any previous writing, it was intended to be an expression of the American mind. . . . All its authority rests then on the harmonizing sentiment of the day, whether expressed in conversation, in letters, printed essays, or in the elementary books of public right, as Aristotle, Cicero, Locke, Sidney, etc. . . . I did not consider it any part of my charge to invent new ideas altogether and to offer no sentiment which had ever been expressed before," he said at another point. The nub of the idea lay in the phrase "*common* sense," which Tom Paine had also employed with the same ample implications not only in the essay bearing that title but in all his revolutionary pamphleteering. Thus such practical letters might draw upon difficult or subtle literary sources but they must communicate common beliefs. Jefferson's stress upon the necessity for ready communication was strong.

Franklin had added the formulation of an esthetic principle in relation to the common or practical arts when he said, "Nothing is good or beautiful but in the measure that it is useful," and in this he had anticipated what we have been accustomed to think of as a modern theory, that of functionalism. That is, that practical arts might have beauty if they perfectly accomplished their ends: in other words, there could be no arbitrary division between the practical arts and the fine arts. Jefferson and Franklin themselves provided proof. The Declaration of Independence, as Jefferson well knew, is an American classic. In his publication of the Indian treaties in Pennsylvania of the middle eighteenth century, Franklin had exceeded a narrow utility which might have trimmed margins, narrowed leads, cramped the headings; such reductions would not have been truly practical for they would have created difficulties for the eye or actual displeasure. Instead, the fine spacings and well-molded type served the useful ends of clarity and magnificently expressed the occasion. Every phase of the ancient ritual imposed by the Indians is rendered with full dignity and an inherent drama. No ornament appears, no excess. These pamphlets are more than fine examples of the printer's art: they become human and immemorial.

In a period of radical and crucial change it was hardly to be expected that these statesmen would be concerned with the arts at all, much less occupied, as some of them were, with the practice of the arts. It must be counted as part of the philosophical breadth into which the nation was born that this was true. No ideas of similar scope were formulated at this time where they might be expected to appear, in the field of criticism. Neither of the two writers who have been called our early major critics, Charles Brockden Brown and Joseph Dennie, had anything comparable to offer. Brown's talent was not critical but creative in a difficult fashion. Dennie was a refined hack who in his *Port Folio* tried to make men of letters serve the government, not in the spacious fashion suggested by Jefferson but as a chorus for the Federalist party. Each lacked ideas. Some of the doubts expressed by Franklin, Washington and the others may at first glance seem straitened, but their concepts of the common or practical arts were radial concepts. They provide touchstones for an approach to American culture in this earliest phase of our national life and perhaps for later phases. Surely the arts belonging to the common life of the time will provide something of a revelation of the life of the new republic.

3

The industrial revolution was not within the ken of these statesmen and indeed lay far in the future as a general movement within the United States, appearing here late. Certainly they had the "mechanic arts" in mind but these were still mainly the handicrafts. Even when a simple mechanics was used, like the potter's wheel or the lathe, the work of the creative hand still played a final part in the national economy. Homespun was common wear. Fabrics for household use, linens, coverlets, rugs, were largely hand-woven, and heavy tools for household use and for the farm were made at the many wayside furnaces or forges. One of these was now much in the popular mind, Valley Forge, whose name has become so drenched in historic experience as to lose its original identity as a place-name. Fragmentary ruins of forges or furnaces of this era showing fine iron doors and magnificent chimneys still may be seen in the back country of New

York, Pennsylvania, Kentucky, and were used for the
making of plowshares, harrows, heavy pots as well as
weathervanes, door latches, and other simple ironwork
long after the machine had come into its own.

These arts were largely rural, as the life of the country
was largely rural. All were in some sense folk-arts, descending by tradition from forms that had been developed
by communal groups living for long in close identity, first
in Europe, then in colonial America. These folk-arts were
not only useful; they constituted a common language of
hand and eye—a familiar speech, which may be read as
any speech is read to discover underlying patterns of
thought, feeling or preoccupation. Differences in idiom
might occur as between the potters of one river valley
and another close by or between housewrights or ship-
wrights in small ports, as in New England, at no great
distance from one another. Their simplicity has sometimes
been read as meagerness, as in some of the small severe
houses perched uncompromisingly on New England hill-
sides, yet this simplicity often expressed a downright
pleasure in stripped forms, and a sensuous delight might
appear in beautifully finished plain surfaces.

Some of these arts were complex, such as the figurehead
carving from New England ports, or the elaborate decorative designs of the Pennsylvania Germans, which had
descended in at least one strain from the intricate manuscript paintings of medieval monasteries and often approached these in symbolic beauty. The six-pointed star,

the lily, the rose, the pomegranate, pairs of doves and
parrots, the figure of a Brunswick princess who perhaps
embodied that worship of the female which has often belonged to primitive societies—these symbols were abundantly familiar in the everyday life of the settlers. The
homeliest tools might show such symbols, and they appeared on objects which were themselves symbolic, the
bride's box, the marriage chest and certificates of birth,
baptism and marriage. Barns that held the harvest were
thus adorned.

All the great ceremonial relationships found expression
in these designs, which were religious and half-pagan in
both origin and feeling. Decades of life among a quite
different folk, the English Quakers, had by no means destroyed the impulse to create them. They were retained,
they were to survive for long even after these people separated and moved down the Valley of Virginia after the
Revolution or farther west in Pennsylvania and into the
Ohio country or to Michigan. The beauty of their art
makes a rich portion of our heritage, and it also has importance for the mind or emotion or basic preoccupations
which it expressed, persisting in spite of other broad concerns which swept the country.

By no means all Pennsylvania German settlers were
concerned with these arts; certain groups quite definitely
were not. Some found their major expression in music.
In the midst of the Revolution, Washington had paused
one night at Bethlehem with only an aide for a companion

and had found pleasure and solace in a concert of cham-
ber-music by the Moravian Brethren. Again, differences
appeared among the musical groups. The musical tradition at Bethlehem was of a different order from that at
Ephrata and elsewhere among the Dunkers, whose primitive hymns were to merge with those of certain English
religious groups or of English origin in the southern states
whose faith was of a similar order.

Much of this music belonged to a sphere that musicians
call "applied music," whose purpose is practical or serviceable as contrasted with the abstract, elaborate, and often
highly complex music which we call "composed." It had
an independent existence of its own. Simple in its forms,
such applied music was used to carry a declaration of
faith, an admission of sin, a hope of heaven. It could
swing a story or provide marked figures for dancing. It
had often been created as an accompaniment for work,
to ease or lighten or hasten a common task by its rhythm
and some absorbing simple tale. In the colonial era and
long afterward, ballads retained this association with
weaving, spinning, cornhusking. Nor was such balladry
confined to a noble inheritance from England and Scot-
land; it was freshly created. Franklin's literary career had
begun at fourteen with the writing of a ballad on the
unhappy death of a lighthouse-keeper and his family,
which he managed to have printed as a broadside and
hawked about the streets of Boston; and familiar episodes
from the French and Indian War were made into ballads.

We listen to these ballads now emerging ghostlike out of the past, but two hundred years ago or even less they brought their immediate lively memories or connotations. They were in a sense serviceable affairs, telling people something they wanted to know or wanted to say or sing or chant. The story might not be new, but if it endured it was likely to be inwrought with association or symbolic meaning, which made affirmations or denials of life or love or death in common terms.

Not only for the telling of stories but for many purposes verse had made a common language all through the colonial era. Both the literate and the illiterate had some command of it. Verse was a spirited mode of popular communication or address, whether it set forth an argument or launched a satire or mourned the passing of a citizen. Broadside verses had been published in increasing abundance on all themes, cresting high, widely distributed, often flowing into song, particularly during the Revolution. Rhythm, as Gummere has said, provides the simplest form of social consent, and the rapid pounding tetrameters and pentameters with their emphatic rhymes could draw a community together, express its dominant thoughts and emotions and make these contagious. Verse used in this fashion belonged to the realm of literature with a purpose—practical letters—as did the related forms of oratory, pulpit eloquence and pamphleteering. The intent of all these forms was to stir, instruct, reprove, applaud—and to establish social communication.

Some of these practical arts might have only what Franklin called "utility under particular circumstances." They were popular, and perhaps transitory; and for the most part "popular" is considered a disparaging word, while "folk" is draped with quaintness and sentiment and colored by the romantic word "Elizabethan." Yet the Scotch and English ballads which with such wearisome emphasis have been given this designation by no means all originated in that great period. A large number of others, many of them of exceptional poetic quality, represent an infiltration of popular English music-hall ballads or street-songs of the seventeenth and eighteenth centuries. These were appropriated for common use and sometimes altered in musical or verbal idiom through use and became part of the common life, while their origins were forgotten. Folk-life is a continuous process whose dominant forms of expression take shape first of all through popular acceptances. Even in its more primitive phases this must have been true. Folk-speech, music, expression in all the arts sprang out of what was greatly popular, and what was instinctively and sometimes perhaps waywardly preserved as a common possession. It is when these popular choices become deeply rooted and are free forms of expression and communication that they become folk-arts. It is then that the social group which has accumulated such forms becomes a folk.

Sentiment has been lavished upon the folk: a prevailing idea has been that the folk are simple, untutored, innocent and rooted in some secluded bit of countryside far from urban centers. But, as we have seen, the decorative art of the Pennsylvania Germans was often highly intricate, with a maze of symbolism; nor were these people illiterate in the main. They set up presses almost immediately after their arrival here and produced a great overflow of German imprints that were widely cherished. Franklin knew them well at Lancaster and sometimes printed English translations for them. None the less they were a folk, held closely together by deeply set unities of thought, emotion and custom which had become instinctive. They were not even a fixed geographic group, for they soon began to spread into new territory, mingling with other groups, altering some of their ways of expression yet maintaining certain dominant forms. Certain of these had digressed from the main stem of their origins in the Palatinate when these people settled here. Their spacious handsome clusters of buildings scattered through rich valleys in eastern Pennsylvania were patterned in the main after primitive rural German farm-buildings, but almost at once adaptations and changes developed, not only because of the increasing use of wood rather than stone but in structure and arrangement both within and without. But the new forms were fairly homogeneous. Even though these farms were widely scattered and there was not a great deal of obvious intercommunication between them, they approximated a bold common style which remained a folk-style.

Such alterations had taken place widely in our colonial era. The usual picture is of closely knit racial groups maintaining their original unities for many years after their first settlement and altered only when the first great waves of migration westward began. It is often said, for example, that the basic stock of New England was mainly English and tenaciously remained so, yet from an early day a French strain was mixed in. The lineage not only of the silversmith Paul Revere but of many others of French descent who practiced crafts or otherwise mingled closely with the common life may be sifted out of the records. Irish immigration to New England was fairly large from the end of the seventeenth century. The fiery Protestant patriot Matthew Lyon from Vermont represented one of its aspects, but there were many other individuals who mixed anonymously with the communal life of the New England towns and the back country, casting away their Gaelic names and their Catholic faith. Traces of Dutch and German settlers may be found; and the outcome was an alteration away from the original English stem. The French and the Irish strains perhaps were more articulate and expressive than the basic English stock and may have accounted in part for the emergence of a new folk character, the Yankee, who somewhat resembled an English prototype, the Yorkshireman, but who was more mobile, livelier, sharper than the English folk-figure. Dry, drawling, shrewd, with a look and lingo of his own, he emerged as a type a little before the Revolution and was celebrated in a song that became its gay rallying cry, "Yankee Doodle." The jigging tune suggests some of the complexity of the Yankee character, and it may also serve to dispel a pervasive myth, that the Puritans suppressed all music except for the psalms, nasally intoned, and that dancing was rigorously ruled out. "Yankee Doodle" would never have started up in New England with such vivacity if dancing had had no place there—dancing which was distinctly of the folk.

Folk-ways of a new order had developed in New England, and we begin to discern these as we place the Yankee figure in the spare small houses that had almost the quality of abstract sculpture, as we begin to see him in taverns or on New England roads in the midst of a horse-trade, or follow him out farther and farther with his peddler's pack into the new western country, retaining his character closely even though he was on the move and though he sometimes settled far from the place of his origin.

Nothing is static in such social groups. Unities that hold them together in one phase may dissolve, while new patterns of common expression may arise. Yet certain broad identities have appeared in folk-expression, as toward an uncompromising directness whether in the building of a house or the painting of a portrait. Symbolism tends to dominate folk-expression, though this may be partially hidden with a strong drift toward poetry. A simple formalism is likely to appear, whether in the decorations on a stoneware jug or in the iterated musical patterns of a ballad. Yet it will be well not to limit the outcome too closely, even as to a prevailing folk-use of the practical arts or handicrafts, or a tendency of the folk to develop in rural or out of the way places. We might find these factors changing.

As to the innocence of the folk, surely this is not inherent. On the contrary, what may be called folk-evil has been a positive force. Folk-evil was present in our colonial settlements from an early period, drawing upon a common inheritance of medieval beliefs in daemonic powers, colored by an infiltration of Indian faith in strange earth spirits, and shaped by the terror of the wilderness. These forces found expression in the concentrated madness of the early religious persecutions of New England and the witchcraft delusions spread through the latter half of the seventeenth century: the influence of Indian beliefs upon the episodes in Salem has been made abundantly clear. These outbreaks have been sufficiently discussed from the point of view of religious intolerance, but not enough as cumulative folk-obsessions, which found other milder outlets in old ballads of magic and witchery and in many minor pagan beliefs and practices. The underlying beliefs and psychic disturbances rose and fell and took manifold forms in successive decades. They gathered new strength from the tortuous introspections induced by Jonathan Edwards and burst into mass hysteria under Whitefield. These outbreaks in which men, women and children

sobbed, confessed, fainted, fell into contortions and became abased, were considered visitations of supernatural
forces. Nor did this folk-sequence by any means belong
only to New England: witch-hunting, though rarely mentioned, occurred in Pennsylvania and Virginia; later Wesley stirred the obscure torment of the revival in the South,
and Whitefield carried his dark fire all the way northward
from Georgia along the Atlantic coast. Throngs listened
to Whitefield as he spoke in the open fields near Philadelphia, and Franklin, who heard him on their outskirts,
thought his swinging oratory was like music. It cast a
strange spell to which even those who resisted his doctrines often yielded, falling into a trance-like anguish
that was so widespread it may be called communal in
its effects.

Even during the Revolution when the common mind
seemed to be wholly engaged with the political and economic causes at issue, these forces were potent. From
1777, for several years, western Massachusetts was visited
again and again by the sweep of revivals of the most
primitive character, as if a kind of common madness su-
perseded any of these considerations, even the issue of
the war itself. In small villages and in thinly populated
rural areas these revivals grew to a culminating intensity
under the leadership of obscure traveling evangelists who
were able to play upon isolation, ignorance and a hoarded
collection of fears, hatreds and ancient half-pagan beliefs.

"Your people, sir—your people is a great *beast*,"

Hamilton said, and the statement has been frequently execrated because of its implied distrust of democracy. Whitefield had told the throngs who listened to him that they were half-beasts, half-devils, and had persuaded them that this was true. These obsessions were part of widespread folk-experience which had by no means ended when the young nation emerged. They had found their own patterns of expression in oratory, song and the social ritual of the revival. These had become deeply channeled and might spread to other imaginative forms. Creative forces sometimes flow from the dark daemonic as well as from loftier or gentler emotions.

4

A philosophy as to the popular or folk-arts was gradually being formulated in Europe during the long period of our first exploration and colonial settlement—a philosophy that reached definition at about the time when Franklin and the others were expressing their views as to the place of such arts in the new nation. This philosophy had mainly to do with literature but it had a wider application.

This philosophy began as a dream of the golden age, and was first voiced in western Europe by Montaigne in an essay on the unlikely subject of cannibals. Specifically there was only one "cannibal," a native South American who had been brought to France by an explorer and was lodged in the house of Montaigne's friends. From the slight barbaric songs of this "cannibal" Montaigne evolved a theory as to what he called *poésie populaire*, by which he meant primitive poetry or song, with the conclusion that the communal life from which it sprang was pure and idyllic. This hopeful concept lay dormant until 1723 when Giambattista Vico extended it to form a base for his theory of history. From a primitive folk-wisdom, he argued, were derived other more complex forms of social wisdom: all mankind passed through three stages of thought, the intuitive, the metaphysical, the scientific, but the primitive was basic. Societies should look back upon this and learn from this phase of racial experience and attempt to recover its pristine freshness.

In his famous early essay on the arts and sciences, the *Discours*, written in 1750, Rousseau carried this idea into a form which had a broad currency: it was repeated in his *Lettre à D'Alembert*. In these comparatively slight works he first stated his belief that primary values had been lost through civilization, that the arts had become decadent as a result and should be abandoned in their contemporary forms, and that the hope of the human race lay in a return to what he called the natural man. Some of these ideas were exemplified by Rousseau's own efforts in music and the theater, wherein he attempted to portray the naturalness and gaiety of the unspoiled rural or provincial character—the folk-character.

Herder next took up the theme. Despising the polite verse of his day, he insisted that it was to the folk rather than to literary sources to which poets must turn, and he urged them to listen to the speech and the song of peasants in the villages and farmsteads and to explore the long accumulations of such expression wherever these might be found. Beginning with his youthful *Fragmente* in 1767, he constructed a theory as to the nature of culture, insisting that the folk-arts laid a base for the fine arts in form, spirit and expression, that folk-forms were the essential forms in any communal group, and that these tended to shape and color sophisticated or conscious art even when they were not specifically drawn upon. He was concerned less with genius or the eventual masterpiece than with the texture of communal experience and expression. In his *Ideen zur Philosophie der Geschichte der Menschheit* (1784-1791), he argued that history should portray the many layers of the cultures of peoples rather than the peaks of achievement. He believed that the basic folk-cultures differed one from another and became concentrated in distinctive national patterns.

But a mild nostalgia quickly took the place of Herder's bold creative concept of the folk as a living wellspring of poetry and song. This was brought about mainly through the selective work of Schlegel and the Grimms, whose explorations of folklore and folk-song had great value but who developed to an extreme the romantic concept of primitive or folk-life which had first been touched upon by Montaigne. Antiquarianism began to cast its long insidious spell, and inquiries as to the folk-arts came to be regarded as minor excursions into the pretty or the quaint. Herder's major theory was to be used to some extent by Eichhorn, Buckle, and later by Guyau; it became indeed part of that tissue of thought in the nineteenth century which regarded society as an organism. But his challenging concept of folk-life as fundamental and his contention that the folk-arts laid a base for the fine arts have never been fully explored.

Some of this long stream of ideas reached these shores, first of all those of Rousseau. The ports of entry here for Rousseau's works have always been difficult to trace, but at least part of the argument of the *Discours* and the *Lettre à D'Alembert,* that which said that the arts had become hopelessly decadent in the service of despotisms, was reflected by John Adams when he wrote so furiously on this theme, though he would never have accepted Rousseau's underlying belief that man is naturally good or that the prime cause of social decadence was inequality; and there is no evidence that Adams had read either of these works. Since these ideas of Rousseau were at once widely and controversially discussed on the continent, undoubtedly in some form they reached these shores, perhaps at an early date. In the same general fashion Herder's concept of cultures as distinctive and national must have reached us with an influence the more reverberant because a new nation whose framework was obviously new was being founded. Herder's theory as to basic folk-cultures might have been expected to find a response here, since it was essentially democratic, but it seems to have created no ripple in this early period; indeed none occurred until some of the transcendentalists and later Walt Whitman saw the major implications of this theory. Even they touched upon it lightly with nothing more than a warm expectation that the arts might come from that general mass known as the people. Herder's special view of the folk-arts was left untouched; indeed no theory as to our culture has been more widely accepted than that which stated that we have lacked folk-expression except for a few fading, vestigial remnants brought here from Europe. Mournful critiques have been written on this theme. In the last ten years suddenly everything that is quaint or exaggerated is folk; but even so the idea of a continuous life of the folk running through the history of the nation has not as yet become a salient idea, nor have possible relationships of the folk-arts to the fine arts seemed basic.

Another concept altogether has dominated approaches to our culture, that of the importance of the peaks of achievement, of the masterpiece, the influence of genius and the fine arts as a final index quality of a culture. With this concept has been joined the far-reaching idea of the arts as luxuries.

5

These ideas also have had a long history which has run almost parallel with the early history of our country. They developed as a part of the Renaissance concept of the gentleman, first in Italy, then in England, when a broad margin of wealth in the commercial cities produced men who had leisure to cultivate their talents. The concept of the gentleman was one of the great archetypal concepts of a great period, embodying the ideal of a harmonious life in which all the creative gifts with which man is endowed might be fully developed: the gentleman was not merely the painter, the sculptor, the musician, the scientist, he was many-sided and expressive, using all the arts for the enrichment of life—sometimes only for his own life, but often for the life about him. Sir Philip Sidney with his social philosophy and his many-sided esthetic concerns was the perfect flower of this idea, but it must be noted that the perfect flowers were rare. The powerful agency of money upset the fine balances belonging to this ideal: not only the gentleman but the new man of wealth appeared in the Renaissance, who if he could not practice the arts could buy them. Because many of the new gentlemen derived at no great distance from the artisan class and wished to leave this behind, they disparaged the homely practical arts and the homely crafts. For the rich

patron the arts were no longer common or broadly prac-
tised as in the rural feudalisms of the Middle Ages. They
became an adornment, a symbol of wealth, a mode of
display that Veblen was to call "conspicuous waste," and
thus something which could be added to or subtracted
from life but not an inherent or necessary part of it.
Under such patronage the practice of the arts became
highly elegant and highly conscious. If Sir Philip Sidney
was the pattern of the gentleman, the same period saw
Lyly with his *Euphues*, the perfect pattern of gentility or
sheer dalliance with words, the absurd extreme of luxury
writing, with all vitality nicely filtered away. The genteel
tradition in literature, so often considered a modern and
even an American invention, may be said to have begun
with Lyly. In the latter Renaissance and the period which
followed all the arts became fine or refined arts. The
sound Latin phrase *bonae literae* dropped from use. Not
the good, the life-giving elements in literature but its possible beauty was stressed: literature became *belles lettres*,
a phrase which could not be applied to the writings of
Marlowe or Shakespeare, which indeed were under a
cloud. The drama of the Restoration arose, the polished
drama of a small class of gentlemen or would-be gentlemen.

Paradoxically the Reformation, which tended to give
dignity to the common man, was also an influence in de-
taching art from the ruck of common life. Its profound
result was to throw the individual upon his own resources

—spiritual, intellectual and material, to separate him from broad established unities. Not only was the individual given sole responsibility for his eternal fate, but, particularly under the guidance of Calvinism, he was cast into a complex and bewildering inner sphere, that of analytical self-scrutiny. No doubt this process would have developed if Luther and Calvin had never lived; it may even be argued that the Reformation arose because of an inevitable drift of the exploratory human spirit toward inner complexities rather than that the Reformation created them. Certainly, too, these preoccupations extended the sphere of human experience and human expression.

The resultant arts possessed exquisite values which we would not do without. They were earthy in Donne, obscurely passionate in Vaughan, richly speculative as in the writings of Sir Thomas Browne. But it is well to see that their elaborate verbal embroidery and conceits are at the farthest possible remove from common or communal expression. It was as if the mind of Hamlet—a mind which the many can in some sense understand—had retired to a formal garden containing a maze cut in fantastic shapes, or to a small gay pergola set deeply within such a garden. These were final refinements in literature, and they occurred at a cost, for they tended still further by the inevitable inner retreat to separate the artist or writer from the broader streams of the common life.

In the later seventeenth century the inevitable transition from *belles lettres* to "polite letters" occurred under a rich patronage. Not all this writing was genteel, but it tended toward gentility. The perfect example is Addison, who must be measured both by his own writing and by that far-spreading phenomenon known as Addisonian prose. Urbane, detached, distinctly minor, this prose displayed within its small well-tended enclosures themes that were intimate but not disturbing, contrived for a limited audience, for those who had leisure to spend their minds mulling over the oddities and quiddities of human character or behavior. This was luxury writing in an appealing form. Though it appeared within the newly developed magazine which seemed to put it into general circulation, its leisured audience remained small and the subscribers distinctly regarded themselves as patrons.

It is true that beneath these lightly balanced sentences lurked a dynamism. The English periodical essay was to open the way for far more vigorous manifestations of the creative spirit in the novel, but this prose also quickly crystallized into a genteel style that was to be preserved for generations as the very apogee of English style and passed inevitably to its final fate as the purely polite essay, a high and lasting example for small *littérateurs* and worshipful schoolmasters.

Further cleavages in the arts had developed as patrons in an earlier period ranged farther and farther afield, if not for a "pillage of the past," at least for a plunder of the arts of other lands. In the England of the Renaissance a simple native art of fresco had been blotted out by importations of both painters and paintings from the continent, and these importations continued through the seventeenth century. What happened to English music, which had been exquisite and varied if not yet deep and rich, has been suggested by Vaughan Williams, who says that when power was attained by uncultured groups and "the practice of art was considered unworthy of a gentleman," the result was that foreigners were hired to produce music, "from which in turn followed the corollary that the type of music which the foreigner brought with him was the only type worth having, and that the very different type of music which was being made at home must necessarily be wrong."

The slow beginnings, the simple, humble, homely phases of native British arts dropped out of consideration. British folk-painting and folk-sculpture have remained unknown territory to this day. When Cecil Sharp began the study of British folk-song at the beginning of the present century he encountered extraordinary difficulties because the field had suffered so profound a neglect. There were exceptions: folk-ballads were collected early in the eighteenth century, and *The Beggar's Opera,* produced in 1728, was proof of a lively interest in song that was popular or vulgar in the true sense. Hogarth, with his coarse and common themes and his portrayal of common people, revealed a vigorous independent native strain which had nothing to do with the arts as luxuries.

This is not to exalt the common arts or common themes

over the luxury arts or to declare that a rich patronage strangled the creative impulse. The history of the arts in Europe is strewn with examples to the contrary. New forms were sometimes created by the very existence of vast wealth, as in the finer passages of that gay and spirited complex decoration known as *rococo*. Nor were importations always a matter of mere plunder. Native forces sometimes made themselves felt through alien hands: the art of Holbein, for example, underwent subtle changes on English soil as did that of other artists from the continent who worked there. Yet under the system of patronage, professional groups arose whose skills were no doubt heightened by specialization but who inevitably retreated into private worlds. The Renaissance gentleman with his many-sided use of his talents was succeeded by the *literati*, men of wealth and leisure who sedulously cultivated the art of letters as a luxury, a class whose absence here Jefferson noted without regret. The *dilettante* appeared, who was concerned with the more delicate fringes of esthetic expression. The Society of the Dilettanti was formed in 1732 and continued for many years by young Englishmen who wished to extend the pleasures they had derived from the grand tour; in particular their interests tended toward a light study of the classics. They built club rooms on the classic model, with the figure of Bacchus as a sculptured device which was appropriate since they were inclined to be bibulous; and they made the important decree that the President should wear a scarlet Roman toga.

The extended spell of the classic ideal, first taking shape in the Renaissance with sprawling vigor in England, declining, then greatly revivified in the mid-eighteenth century, meant a fixing of norms or patterns in the arts and their further separation in practice and in critical approach one from another. When through excavation an ancient civilization was disclosed in Herculaneum and Pompeii, each of the arts stood forth as a distinct form; with this full picture in view it was perhaps inevitable that these should seem the apogee of all art. These ideas acquired precision and refinement through Stuart and Revett's *Antiquities of Athens,* which became an English source-book for architecture and decoration, and through the critiques of Winckelmann and Lessing. It was Lessing who gave a final impetus to the separation of the arts by his contention, in which he followed Aristotle, that each of these had a separate function and should be kept rigorously distinct. Clustered with these within a brief span of years—between 1750 and 1760—were other studies which sought to establish classic purity of form and equable balance as the final quality to be desired in all art, Burke's essay *On Our Ideas of the Sublime and the Beautiful* foremost among them.

This period represented the first great rise of the critical spirit as applied to the arts. Perhaps at no time either before or since have such certainties existed as to what art is, what the separate arts are, what their qualities should be; and, since wealth alone could acquire the impressive manifestations of classic art, the view of the arts as luxuries received further confirmation. It was inevitable that these ideas should have their influence here: they were the conscious ideas of the arts with which our culture began, streaming down from the late Renaissance. Their full emergence in the mid-eighteenth century coincided with the first great period of mercantile expansion in this country, that is, with the first broad accumulation of colonial wealth, and their print went deep.

6

When Washington and the others expressed a belief that the fine arts were luxuries which the new nation could not afford, they must have had in mind the poverty following in the wake of the Revolution, the dislocations of internal trade, even the devastation wrought by Tarleton in Virginia. Yet many individuals and even whole communities were far from being poor as the Revolution ended.

In the full sense of the word Boston, Providence, New York, Philadelphia, Charleston had long since been urban, with a generous development of advanced forms of civic life and a patronage of painting, architecture, music, and —in the case of New York and Charleston—of the theater:

in such respects these cities compared favorably or more than favorably with English ports of the same size. Smaller cities, Newburyport, Newport, Perth Amboy, and a scattering of inland villages had shown a persistent interest in the fine arts. The towns of Salem and Annapolis, since they were neither large nor small and since their history was closely intertwined with that of the whole nation, revealed the strength and breadth of these interests.

More than half the privateers of the Revolution were said to have come from Salem. They had kept sea lanes open, maintained our sea-power, and brought in essential supplies for the army. Such commanders as Captain Jonathan Harraden could bluff or attack under cover of darkness or make his ship show a clean pair of heels when outclassed in guns or size: the records of Salem shipping are packed with such exploits. Every man aboard had a gambling chance to win substantial money as the first to descry an enemy sail or to board an enemy ship, and both officers and men received shares when the ships returned from Bilbao, Cadiz, Guadeloupe or Jamaica and the spoils were sold at auction. When peace came the *Grand Turk,* belonging to Elias Hasket Derby, a ship with many prizes to her credit, sailed away again almost at once, returning with teas, silks and ware from Canton in her hold; she had unlocked the door to the China trade. Two years later Captain Jonathan Carnes discovered an unknown portion of the Sumatra coast where pepper, camphor, and spices were to be had in quantities, packed the hold of his brig with these, and brought home a fortune, thus opening another phase of richly profitable commerce.

In Salem the air of well-tended latitude lay everywhere as the Revolution ended. With its deeply enclosed harbor, its neighboring inlets, coves and converging streams, its ample wharves and great warehouses, the town faced outward toward the Atlantic like a small, well-fortified spacious entrenchment, secure in its power. Salem men had long shown a liking for fine houses: many of the early dwellings with gambrel roofs, spacious rooms, airy interiors still remained standing at the time of the Revolution, and a succession of others had been built, such as the handsome Cabot-Endicott-Low mansion. In 1766 John Adams was saying that he found in Salem houses which were "the most elegant and grand I have ever seen in any of our maritime towns." By 1782 the village was being transformed into a town of scale and dignity and was under the hand of Samuel McIntire, who was beginning to build houses for the Derbys, Crowninshields, Boardmans, Forresters and others, as well as a series of fine public buildings.

The earlier dwellings had shown the simple pineapple carved over a doorway or the humble cod placed 'scutcheon-wise on its staircases, but in response to a new opulence the interior woodwork of these new mansions began to bloom under McIntire's hand with exquisitely detailed moldings in the classic patterns, festoons of drapery, overflowing cornucopias, sprays of laurel and grape, and baskets of luxuriant flowers and fruit. These houses were furnished with rich rugs, brasses, porcelains, exotic carvings, and sometimes strange gods from the Far East. Portraits by Smibert, Greenwood, Blackburn, Copley hung on Salem walls as did the work of many admirable journeymen painters; nor were the subjects of such portraits drawn only from families who had acquired great fortunes. Mates, masters, and lesser men were also delineated—highly individualized characters who still look out firmly from old canvasses. John Becket, a caulker and shipwright, on a trip to Florence was portrayed by an Italian artist: in a blue coat, a pale yellow waistcoat, a frilled shirt, with a pair of dividers in his hand. The portrait still hangs in Salem.

Far in the past lay Salem's turgid psychic history, its gusty dark emotionalism, its severely imposed restrictions upon the forms of faith and personal conduct. By the mid-eighteenth century, dancing masters were welcomed; in 1768 an assembly-room was built by private subscription for balls, and these had a considerable gaiety and sparkle. Some gentlemen of leisure had formed a club for the study of polite letters—the phrase was explicit; and in 1780 the Social Library was established with books imported from London. A great haul of scientific volumes by one of the Cabots' privateersmen during the Revolution made a nucleus for the Philosophical Society, books for which its members offered payment when the war was over. The American Philosophical Society at Philadelphia, founded by Franklin, was the first of its kind founded in this country, that at Salem was second. The library of William Bentley, who came to Salem in 1783, was considered the finest private library in the United States, barring only that of Jefferson.

These pursuits, which meant a margin of leisure and of wealth, were widely spread. Perhaps the society of Salem could not be called entirely democratic; Bentley suggested that Samuel McIntire was not received as an equal in the great houses he built; yet something akin to equalitarianism in the patronage of the arts existed, bred perhaps of shared maritime adventures in the long period and capped by the common cause in the Revolution. Nor was this patronage a mere piling up of plunder from foreign parts: pronounced tastes appeared in the town. Though a considerable number of novels were imported, those of Fielding, Smollett and Richardson, with plays and poetry in real abundance, the turn toward scientific and philosophical works overshadowed these. Though individuals practiced the making of polite verse, far more noticeable was connoisseurship in the plastic and space arts, the highly tangible arts of painting, decoration, architecture. In relation to the town's main occupation of shipping these branching concerns were fused, in the skillful building of ships, the fine carving of ships' figureheads, and the growing occupation with the basic natural

sciences required for a perfection of seamanship. By the
end of the Revolution, Salem had bred a magnificent
series of minor characters out of the sea and its ways; and
the town itself had all the concentrated special lineaments
of a complex individual.

Set near the mouth of the Severn, looking toward the
wide waters of the Chesapeake, Annapolis had also long
been a principal port and had a maritime look; its early
houses, even its churches might have been built by ship-
wrights and perhaps were, so firmly did they rise from
the green folds of a gentle landscape, but its character,
no less explicit than that of Salem, was of a different
order. Near its center stood—and still stands—an ancient
tulip tree under which in 1652 a treaty with the Susque-
hannocks was signed. Even then, before the town was
founded, a concern with government and governmental
power had been forecast. Some forty years later Annapolis
was laid out as the seat of government in Maryland, the
first town in the colonies to be so designed and one of
the first examples of town planning: its radial streets created fine vistas, the portion given to the houses of crafts-
men or mechanics had open spaces for public games, frol-
ics, fairs. With their great walled gardens, their broad
wings, their look of the manor-house, the larger dwellings
of the town seemed to belong to the country, but they
had been built because their owners, many of whom had
large country estates, were concerned with the stream of
political affairs. A capitol building was erected in 1697

and three times rebuilt: the final structure of patterned English brick with a simple porch and a dome constructed as "by an inspired ship's carpenter" was provincial in style, but it was to rank with Independence Hall in Philadelphia and the old State House in Boston as one of the most significant of public buildings in the colonies, a model for others to follow, with a wealth of national associations. The procedures leading to the Declaration of Independence took place there, and it was a meeting-place of the Continental Congress. Washington came to the capitol to lay before the Congress his commission as commander-in-chief, at the end of the Revolution, and there the final treaty of peace was signed a year later. There too were passed the momentous resolutions which led to the writing of the Constitution.

Beginning early, this concern with the forms and the philosophy of government had taken many consistent forms. At least by 1686 the first of a succession of printers had appeared whose first business was the printing of the body of laws. In 1727 William Parks established the famous Maryland *Gazette*, one of the earliest of colonial newspapers, which exerted an influence far outside the boundaries of the town or the colony, and with only one break continued its vigorous, many-sided discussion of public affairs well into the nineteenth century. Nor were these interests confined to the gentlemen of the town or the colony. A portrait survives of a lovely Annapolis lady with a volume of Locke in her lap, which not only sug-

gests ideas that had a far-reaching influence upon the
philosophy of the Revolution but reveals a typical concern of the ladies of Annapolis: though far from being
bluestockings they were noted for what an admiring trav-
eler called "the embellishments of the mind."

These interests were placed in an ample setting of
wealth, of luxury, of the fine arts. If the ladies were as
noted for their interest in intellectual matters, they were
also famous for their devotion to fashion and gay apparel,
their exquisite velvets, silks, laces. These people traveled
in coaches and four, gave great balls, attended races,
hunted over the countryside, and preserved a quaint and
ancient custom from the medieval courts. The gentlemen
tilted for ladies' favors on horseback with lances and
rings. Even now in Maryland this custom survives.

The luxury arts were an inevitable accompaniment of
this existence. Portraits had been brought from England,
others were painted there when their subjects, both men
and women, paid frequent visits there. Annapolis possessed a broader background of purely English painting
than did Salem, but patronage was established there early
for a succession of painters who were either born in the
colonies or allied their fortunes with them—a succession
which just before the Revolution led to the young Charles
Willson Peale, born in Maryland, who was sent to London
for study under West by a group of Annapolis gentlemen.
The finer handicrafts, notably those of the silversmith,
began early in Annapolis. The town provided early sup-

port of the theater. In 1771 one of the early adventurous managers built a charmingly constructed theater to house the performances of his company. The English actor, John Bernard, called Annapolis the Bath of America because of its gaiety, fashion, wit; indeed he found all Maryland "one wide temple of mirth and sociability." Nor were the sources of sociability all imported; Annapolis men and women provided some of them. Their discussions of politics and government were placed in an ample setting of a concern with literature, not all of which could be called polite, some of which sprang directly from Maryland soil. Satirical verse appearing in the *Gazette* was often rudely trenchant as to men, manners and beliefs; and its owner published books by that gross Maryland satirist, Ebenezer Cooke, the author of *The Scot-Weed Factor*. These were amusements of hearty men who had by no means lost a sense of earth; but as the eighteenth century wore on some of the coarser elements were fused away. Essays in the Addisonian manner began to appear in the *Gazette;* before 1750 the Tuesday Club was formed for the study of elegant writing and its practice, as well as for the leisured art of what was called literary conversation. Distinguished guests from other regions were often invited to participate in these exercises, and since Benjamin Franklin was one of them we may hope that they were not altogether lacking in hearty vigor.

7

Any one of our elder statesmen would have known of these pools or pockets of the arts. Franklin had been a guest of the Tuesday Club at Annapolis, John Adams knew Salem well. Any one of them would no doubt have declared that rich men would continue to patronize the fine arts here as elsewhere.

Their final question was not whether Americans would possess the fine arts but whether they could create them; and this question was set against an immediate context. Anticipating Sidney Smith's famous challenge by more than a generation, the Abbé Raynal had declared in his *Recherches Philosophiques sur les Américains* that America had not yet produced one poet, one mathematician, one man of genius in a single art or a single science; and he had contended further that a progressive physical degeneration of both animals and human beings was taking place on American soil. After the publication of the *Recherches*, on an occasion when Raynal was present, Franklin led the conversation around to the Abbé's contentions as to the American physique, then merrily invited the company to stand up; whereupon it appeared that the Americans were all above average stature while the French were "remarkably undersized" and the Abbé himself was "a mere shrimp," as Franklin told Jefferson.

But Raynal's theory as to natural life in America was endorsed by Buffon and other leading European scientists and had a considerable vogue in Europe; even now odd reverberations from it may be met abroad. In this country these conclusions were widely discussed; and the attack cut the deeper because Raynal had been the subject of friendly honor here. Hamilton referred indignantly to Raynal in the *Federalist*. Washington and Jefferson attempted to meet the charges as to American failure in science, saying that Franklin, Rittenhouse and Rush were no mean names. As to genius, Jefferson in his *Notes on Virginia* pointed to Washington. Washington in turn spoke of Jefferson as a genius in the sphere of political thought, and went on to say hopefully that he had heard the works of Jonathan Edwards were used in the study of philosophy at European universities. He seemed almost grateful when Bernard told him that he had never encountered a more refined society than that of Philadelphia. But no one could declare that America had triumphed in the fine arts. "America, though but the child of yesterday, has already given hopeful proofs of genius," said Jefferson, but he was acutely aware of American deficiencies, particularly in painting, sculpture and music.

What was to be done about it? Jefferson himself had contrived an answer when in 1779 he had begun the study of classic architecture in France. Before the Revolution Copley had sailed for England where he was to work for the rest of his days under English patronage.

West, Stuart, Peale, Earl, Pratt had gone abroad to work
or study, and a long procession of other artists and some
writers was soon to begin journeys to the wellsprings of
European culture. The underlying philosophy was well
defined: the finer phases of our culture must derive from
Europe. Nothing could have seemed more obvious. Samuel McIntire was using the designs of the English architect Battey Langley for the buildings by which he was
changing the face of Salem. In Annapolis the volume of
Locke in the lovely lady's lap was symbolical; main
sources of essential American thought were to be found
in Europe. Our early study of science had been linked directly with the Royal Society. Our cultural landscape was
filled with such evidences, nor did they all derive from
England: French, Flemish and German strains could be
traced in our architecture, in the crafts, in music.

Tangible reinforcement was at hand for a powerful
theory, which John Fiske was later to call the "transit of
civilization." This was inevitably accepted in the colonial
era and has been further defined, elaborated and added
to explicitly or otherwise until it stands as a main approach to the study of our culture and even of our political, social and economic history. The theory was that if
we dipped deeply and often enough into the major European streams we might hope to witness their rise among
us. Culture would be achieved by means of "carriers"—
artists, writers, musicians were all "carriers"—both those
who went to Europe to study and came back and those

who migrated from Europe here; and their works might
also be "carriers." The arts would spread much as water
is passed in buckets at a country fire—spilled along the
way no doubt, with much of it lost and perhaps acquiring
a peculiar tang or flavor, if one should taste it. What we
might hope eventually to possess was an extension of
European culture, that is, if the process of diffusion was
not too greatly impaired by forces peculiar to American
life.

For the theory as it has come down the years has been
hedged about by stipulations and darkly colored by dis-
couragement. When our elder statesmen said in substance
that Americans would long be too much occupied to concern themselves with the arts, they were forecasting arguments which were to be repeated again and again through
decades. The vast enterprise of conquering the country
would exclude leisure for the arts: so this major argument
has run. Further, our gross materialism has been said to
have blocked the arts, thwarting the creative impulse,
turning our society away from these refinements. Life on
our successive frontiers has been declared destructive of
these concerns, so raw was its character, so vast the preoccupation there with the mere business of living. Finally
Puritanism is said to have repressed the fine arts, from our
earliest periods, with a pervasive influence against them
which has lasted down to the present day. Sometimes
these charges have become links in a chain: Puritanism

created materialism, both forces were strengthened on the frontier and none of them permitted leisure.

These arguments have culminated in the theory of the "lag." American culture has been viewed as following European culture much as the lady-in-waiting follows the accomplished heroine in *The Critic,* at a distance, gawkily going through some of the same motions but by no means achieving the same grace. This concept of culture has been one of absolutes, which took shape here through the establishment of the classic ideal at precisely the time when our first consciousness of the fine arts emerged, in the second quarter of the eighteenth century. In particular since our literature began to emerge in this period, as the polite essay came into bloom, this minor form became a pattern for our early writers; little magazines were established under a patronage similar to that in England. These small digressions into the field of *belles lettres* had, with similar little excursions into polite verse, already come to occupy a disproportionate place in our scheme of cultural values when our national history began because of the ease with which these little forms could be imitated. Imitation is the core of this concept of culture. Thus because of our main racial sources in Great Britain, because of the common language, and because of the magnificent stream of English literature, it was not unnaturally assumed that ours would be a literary culture. Indeed to this day the word culture in this country is practically synonymous with literary culture, with an emphasis upon *belles lettres,* the more refined and recondite levels of literature, the peaks of achievement.

The result has been that the main approach to our culture has been the segmented literary approach with major efforts going toward the attempt to trace relationships between American literature and English literature, or in a minor fashion between the other arts in America and the British or European arts. Our historical studies are ridden by such efforts, which make one of the simplest, safest forms of scholarship, but which prove nothing at all as to underlying creative forces. No civilization has sprung full-blown into existence without an ancestry. No society has been free from alien or antecedent influences, so common has been the mixing of cultures through migration, conquest and simple loot. Obviously American culture has inherited the general forms of culture developed by Western civilization. If correspondences are sought between the arts in this country and those of Europe it will be easy to find them, in any period. If one looks for a "lag," innumerable instances may be discovered in which the arts have appeared later here than in Europe. But the arts that are mainly derivative are likely to appear slowly, even to be thin and feeble. None of these circumstances suggests anything more than the operation of forces well known in all cultures.

8

The seeds of influence may fall but they may not germinate. Works belonging to other cultures may stir the imagination but not the creative imagination. If the results are a weedy fringe this does not necessarily mean that the soil is poor. It may only be sterile for the particular seeds blown upon it though enriching others. The original use of the word culture contains its most far-reaching idea: culture is tillage, a fertile medium, a base or groundwork inducing germination and growth. Surely a culture is the sum of such growth in terms of expression. Not the separate arts but the whole configuration will tell the story.

"So closely are the several departments of civilization knit together that concentration on any one of them to the exclusion of others is an impracticable undertaking," says Robert H. Lowie, speaking of primitive groups; and his comment on "the mutual dependence of apparently disparate branches of culture" in such groups also applies to more complex societies. In her *Patterns of Culture*, Ruth Benedict says: "A culture, like an individual, is a more or less consistent pattern of thought and action. . . . The whole, as modern science is insisting in many fields, is not merely the sum of all its parts, but the result of a unique arrangement and interrelation of the parts that has brought about a new entity. . . . Anthropologists are turning from the study of primitive culture to that of primitive cultures, and the implications of this change from singular to plural are only just beginning to be evident. The importance of the study of the whole configuration as over against the continued analysis of its parts is stressed in field after field of modern science. . . . It is felt that hardly any trait of culture can be understood when taken out of its general setting."

This was Franklin's idea when he suggested that forms of expression were relative to the society, the places and the times in which they appeared. It is the whole configuration in the particular period which is important, with its special tenacities, currents of thought, contagions of feeling, its dominant arts, whether these are polite or impolite, practical or impractical, whether they slip over surfaces in transitory popular forms or become rooted as patterns of the folk imagination or, more broadly, of the social imagination.

This is by no means to deny the importance of luxuries of the mind or spirit or the luxury arts. Nor is it to deny the place of genius or its peaks of imaginative achievement. But genius is never truly solitary though it is often proclaimed to be so. As Vaughan Williams says, "Its great achievements are the crest of the wave. For every great composer there must be a background of dozens of smaller men." Williams insists that the actual pioneers in a movement are most often inferior in expressive power, because they are plowing new ground with difficulty. Still further he points out that the whole idea of originality, the modern insistence upon the unique individuality of the artist, is of comparatively recent growth.

In a nascent culture such as ours, peaks of achievement have occurred and must have their place, but if our concern is with the whole dimensional pattern minor figures may also become symbols of a dominant creative effort. Not merely the individual but the culture of a group, a town, a region may be significant of main tendencies. Bred as we are and must be in the older cultures, we may sometimes easily miss or fail to appraise the special qualities of our nascent culture. Santayana has said, "The gestation of a native culture is necessarily long, and the new birth may seem ugly to an eye accustomed to some other forms of excellence." Yet the effect of ugliness may be the result of prepossessions, and a special pleasure may often be derived from fresh beginnings, from half-formed yet vigorous new directions.

Whatever the gaps, the mischances, the downright inferiority of some of our early arts, they cannot be considered in the main as first fumblings of mere ambitious imitation. They sprang from a life peculiar to these shores; they were part of a fresh configuration. McIntire used the designs of Battey Langley, but even his early houses in Salem could never be mistaken for English houses deriving from the same source. As his craft developed, as the demands of Salem merchants and shipmasters made themselves felt, his architecture was to move still farther from these originals. The look of the Salem which he largely created was unlike that of any English town: tastes, ideas and homely purposes developing over a long period had created a special design. Though Annapolis could be called the Bath of America, it was nothing like Bath. The whole structure of social life there as well as its appearance was of another order: and if, as contrasted with the formal elegance of Bath, it was provincial, Annapolis also had an easy spaciousness which the English city did not possess. And though Locke was read by the lovely lady and by Thomas Jefferson and many others, surely the influence of this English philosopher burgeoned here in forms of social theory and political revolution which were not English forms.

The Renaissance tradition of the gentleman had long since been perpetuated in the American colonies, but with deviations from the English tradition. Cotton Mather certainly had no kinship with Sir Philip Sidney either as an individual or a type, yet he possessed the exploratory talent, using this at leisure even in the midst of the harsh complexities of colonial life, which marked the character of the gentleman. With Mather, as with others in New England at the same time, a main concern outside the minutiae of religious philosophy was science; and this strain also appeared among the ship-owners and merchants of Salem, who extended the concept of the gentleman within firm and hearty outlines. Zest rather than elegance belonged to them. The gentleman has been most often discerned among the plantation owners of the Southern colonies through a continuation of the cavalier tradition, yet in the South, too, even with the same strong adherence to classicism in its many forms which was a consistent part of the Renaissance idea, differences appeared: as in New England, science was a major concern, together with natural philosophy, as it was called, and the theory of government. Thus the main bias was practical. The supreme example was Jefferson, who came from the uplands and seemed far removed by birth and tradition from the cavalier type, but who moved readily in these fields and was also a practicing architect and a connoisseur in music.

As compared with the rich clusters of the fine arts in Europe, these were spread here a little thinly. In this respect our early culture was cool and frosty rather than luxuriant. Yet no settled section of the country lacked the arts, and this diffusion itself represented a pronounced cultural trait. Instead of the marked concentrations of the arts in London or Paris, this concern had developed in many radial centers along the Atlantic seaboard and even inland, some of them with highly individualized tastes. Our larger cultural pattern, which in so many ways seemed to derive from England, approximated rather the uncentralized patterns of the German kingdoms or the Bohemian provinces.

The scattering which followed upon the founding of

the many separate colonies has often been mentioned, and it is obvious that many rich variables belonging to the older cultures were absent there. In the theory of "transit," this circumstance has been stressed as deprivation, but the constructive effect upon the cultural forces actually planted here has been neglected. Because they appeared in comparative isolation they reverberated like loud voices in an empty room; and they fell into new relationships. Thus the psychological intensities of Calvinism were greatly deepened in the New England colonies as compared with the practice of Calvinism in English communities, which tended to fringe off into groups of a quite different character and thus to become modified. And these peculiar inner intensities fell into conjunction with wholly primitive influences here. All through the colonial period up to the French and Indian War the colonists fought savage foes and even adopted some of their forms of savagery, against a background of this intricate inner quest. Because this quest was highly intellectualized through the minute Calvinist dialectic, surely the conjunction was strange and perhaps explosive: certainly it was powerful, and it constituted a new cultural pattern. Science fell into it, with a further acceleration of intellectual forces, as did the literacy which the Puritans cultivated in order that the individual might use all the resources of religious and theological literature. The effects of literacy were likewise magnified by isolation, with the result that dependence upon the printed word early became a common social trait. All these forces were human, cultural, creative, and they had been put together in new and deeply set arrangements. And while it cannot be sweepingly said that "sky determines," that is, that cultures are basically conditioned by environmental factors, nevertheless these factors were forces mingling with others in our early settlements. Strange horizons, a totally unknown continent, extremes in climate—these created a rigorous and electric medium within which all experience was shaped and colored. Yet there was a lush abundance or its promise everywhere. These forces were all but antiphonal, one set complexly against the other.

Essential patterns of thought, emotion and imagination were freshly twisted, emboldened, pulled into new dimensional forms; and it is the resultant configuration that must concern us rather than the separated parts or their antecedent sources. This is by no means to argue that the parent cultures need not be brought into view. To discover the place of purely imitative strains within the new pattern will be important. In all ways the European cultures provide frames of reference. Their great achievements may, among other things, prevent an over-exaltation of our achievements.

But an overweighing consciousness of the older cultures should not be permitted to dull the sense of new directions in our own. Nothing was fixed or predetermined among the forces at work. In spite of the obvious ties with Britain, in spite of our abundant literacy, in spite of what Emerson was to call our "enormous paper currency of words," perhaps after all the American genius is not literary. Henry James, writing of Hawthorne a hundred years after the nation was founded, thought that it was not. The governing idea that ours is a literary culture, or any similar preconception, may throw our judgments awry. New coalescences in thought, imagination, feeling and creative form were constantly appearing in these earlier days. Instead of the equilibrium that is often considered a requisite for creation in the arts—an idea deriving from the classic ideal—disequilibrium was a major force, because of continual movements toward new frontiers, because of the commingling of groups that often represented different races and different phases of culture and different communal aims. Sudden increases in population were about to take place: that of Baltimore was to double more than twice between 1775 and 1800 because the city formed a water-bounded gateway to the Blue Ridge and thence to the West.

Yet we cannot say that these sudden expansions meant cultural disintegration on the frontier or in those territories along the seaboard from which the newer frontiers were in part derived, as a common theory has it, or even that the "transit" of elements from the European cultures was thinner, the greater the distance from their source. In many instances whole groups passed as "carriers" directly from Europe into the new West—from France, Switzerland, Germany. In any event social equilibrium may not be the only condition for sustaining the arts. Motion itself may perhaps become a medium in which they can flourish. Not disintegration but the nascence of new forms may have taken place on these farther boundaries. If fresh alignments could take place in the first Atlantic settlements, surely these could occur as frontiers were moved inland.

Nor can the effect of other forces be taken for granted as destructive of our culture, for example, the Puritanism that is so frequently referred to. In point of fact, this theory crumbles in the nearer view: a cluster of proofs to the contrary appeared in the climactic period when the country was emerging from the Revolution, all of them with clear antecedents. If the theory as to the Puritan suppression of the arts were true, painting might have been expected to develop first where the Puritan influence was absent, in the Southern colonies; yet its most vigorous native growth was in New England and in Pennsylvania, where the puritanical Quakers flourished. In the application of this theory, the forms most stressed have been the drama and the novel, but the curious fact is that the first play with an American subject, *Ponteach,* was written by a New Englander. Satirical plays written by New Englanders during the Revolution created a major direction of our early drama. A New Englander, Royall Tyler, wrote the first American play with an American subject to be publicly performed, *The Contrast.* And the slight narratives that appeared before and soon after the Revolution, which are generally considered the beginnings of the American novel, were also written by New Englanders. In other words, if these several arts failed in a vigorous early growth, this circumstance can hardly be laid at the door of the Puritans.

As for the long course of argument, advanced frequently by Marxist critics and others, that our culture has been destroyed or diminished by a persistent materialism, a primary instance to the contrary is Hakluyt's *Voyages,* which in the broad sense may be considered our own, since life on this continent was in a fashion cradled by these writings: they recorded early explorations to this continent, and they led to others and were deeply cherished by our early colonists. Horizons were widened beyond the immediate wilderness by them, and they became a prototype for a literature relating to the exploration of new country over successive periods.

The *Voyages* were long considered a product of the high literary imagination at work upon sea-going adventures of the Tudor and Elizabethan eras, but we know now that their purpose was—to put it grossly—commercial. No one of them was concerned with the cloudland of faery that had often been described within their pages: they were written for the benefit of traders and explorers who roamed the seas on behalf of the great mercantile houses. A triumphant materialism gave rise to the splendor of this prose. Though the *Voyages* may be read as Homer is read, they belong quite strictly to the realm of practical letters. This is not to say that materialism may never be destructive, only that the sweeping theory will not stand.

The concern of Franklin, Washington, Jefferson and Adams with the arts as common utility provides a broad chart for an approach to American culture which by no means excludes the fine arts or the derivative forms of expression but which keeps the center of gravity within that social complex out of which the arts must spring. As for the several arts—using the word in the inclusive eighteenth-century sense to include the crafts and sciences, if we view them separately, it will not be with Lessing's idea of rigid demarcations but with the purpose of achieving some measure of simplicity in a complex field and with the belief that stresses upon one form or another may themselves be significant as revealing social aptitudes or tendencies. The main values must remain human values. In segmented views of a culture the great human themes are sometimes forgotten: life, death, love, nature. What did our young nation do with them? In what sphere were its hopes, fears and aspirations most articulate? If beauty was achieved, in what did its quality mainly consist? Esthetic questions may also be human questions. The span of time between 1783 and 1825, covering more than a generation, should reveal continuities in our basic social character, or, if breaks occur, these may be salient since this era represents a crucial phase in our history.

The Rise of Theatricals

I. THE INDIAN BACKGROUND

HARDLY had Columbus brought back to Europe tidings of his first voyage when a fanciful woodcut was made in Augsburg showing a cluster of Indians wearing feather headdresses and decked with precious stones. Portions of a human being were hung on a limb in preparation for a feast.

Nearly a century later John White, the governor of Roanoke, made a series of exquisite water-color drawings in which he noted flora and fauna of the new continent with some of the aboriginal inhabitants. Engraved by de Bry, they passed into a considerable European currency.

Early in the seventeenth century small figures in wood called "black boys" were placed outside apothecaries' shops in London to advertise tobacco: they were the first of a long lineage of shop-signs continuing to this day in the last of the cigar-store Indians, now shabbily and obscurely. With tobacco and later cigars in an outstretched hand they symbolized the fact that the white men had first received the assuaging gift from the Indian.

The symbolic, the fanciful invaded many of the colonial

writings on the Indian; yet John Smith, Bradford, Thomas Morton and many others studiously sought to record their experiences and their knowledge of the Indian in terms of fact. A great body of writing developed in all the colonies whose intent was historical. The stories of captivities experienced by white men and women alone made a small literature. In *The History of the American Indians* (1775), James Adair advanced the theory that the Indians were the lost tribes of Israel, but, in spite of this flight of the imagination, which was to obtain widespread credence and to be repeated and embroidered many times, the book was a record, particularly as to the character and customs of the Cherokees and the Chickasaws: even the lofty hypothesis was formulated with a scientific purpose, to account for the origins of the race. Some of these records were practical; some were early ventures in anthropology. Adair was an Irish trader, a man of education, instinctively a scholar, who poured into his book a genuine passion for the wilderness. Few of these writings were wholly detached. Some of them were harsh. A positive freshness belongs to many of them, as if the momentous drama being enacted between the two races in this morning of the new world were instinctively realized.

In most of these works dramatic episodes were outlined in terms of character and dialogue with an interplay of action between the Indians and the whites. This relationship found its most complete expression in the Indian treaties, set down in amplitude as early as 1677. These treaties were essentially plays—chronicle plays—recording what was said in the parleys, including bits of action, the exchanges of gifts, of wampum, the smoking of pipes, the many ceremonials with dances, cries and choral songs. Even the printed form of the treaties was dramatic: the participants were listed like a cast of characters, and precise notations were made as to ceremonial action. Symbolic phrases were used to seal promises, even to raise questions.

In the Iroquois treaties the very beautiful ceremonial beginning "At the wood's edge" from the Iroquois book of rites was invariably introduced. On one occasion Takanunty, an Onondaga chief, courteously told Conrad Weiser that the Six Nations could not go to Williamsburg to meet the southern Indians to make a treaty "as there is no road to that place. We never travel through bushes to treaties of peace. It is too dangerous, and we have no fire at Williamsburg. . . . Such a thing cannot be done in a corner, it must be done by public fire." This contention would have been accepted by leaders in all the Indian tribes because the fire and the road were established symbols, because ceremonials springing from deeply rooted communal experience must be preserved, because human dignity was a force that was widely understood.

Indian speech was characteristically grave and rhythmic, but it attained a sharp and witty realism in the discussion of rum, trappers, traders and white trickery. The Indian style of address was generally accepted and used by the white men, even to the sly introduction of humor, and the Indians imposed their own rituals of procedure.

The participants were proprietors, agents, interpreters: Thomas Penn—whose father William was frequently mentioned—Franklin, Croghan, Conrad Weiser, Peter Randolph. They included such sachems as the Oneida chief, Shikellamy, Teedyuscung, chief of the Delawares, the famous Onondaga orator Canasatego and Tamamend—Tammany. The Penobscots, the Tuscaroras, the Senecas, the Mohawks, all the most popular tribes were represented in these transactions and the chief came to them attended by a crowd of warriors, women, even children.

These treaties were formulated in most of the colonies, as far to the west as Fort Pitt.

"Forest diplomacy" in all ways was cast against wide horizons. The Indians—particularly the powerful Six Nations—held the balance of power between the English and the French; they played cunningly upon it: this circumstance made the great fulcrum upon which their successive actions turned. The early treaties are linked by this underlying theme, but they were also bound by a tragedy plainly revealed as tribe after tribe retreated westward.

Some fifty of these treaties are known to have been printed: their cycle has epic proportions as well as an epic theme. In the exact sense they are incomparable; nothing like them exists in our own literature or any other. Quite strictly they belong to practical letters; they were created for practical ends, yet these products of two races were poetry of a high order. In their own time they had a wide currency not only because of their political significance but for their rich episodes, their bold portraiture, their singular fragments of human history. Franklin, who published thirteen of them, had three hundred copies of the Lancaster Treaty of 1774 struck off for sale in England as a literary curiosity, and William Parks also printed this stately treaty—one of the finest and most dramatic of them all—for an audience in Virginia and Maryland concerned with literary as well as historical values.

The treaties have never been included within the sequence of our drama, yet they are in truth our first American plays. The first of them antedates by some eighty years Godfrey's *The Prince of Parthia,* usually considered the first American play, a poetic drama that seems narrow, stilted and remote by comparison with any one of the treaties—a piece of philosophical elegance by a would-be *littérateur.* That the treaties could be matched in poetic or imaginative values by individual effort in their own time was hardly to be expected: they were traditional, communal, they expressed values that had long been accumulated. They were part of an evolving sequence that was to endure long past the period of the Revolution. Yet they had a powerful expressive influence upon the drama: *Ponteach,* the first American play on a native subject, used a theme related to theirs with something of their ritual. Though the language lacks the poetic Indian concentration, some of the typical symbolism of the treaties recurs in the play. Robert Rogers, its author, was in no sense literary though he could write a good straightforward prose. He was a frontiersman, a great strapping giant with a bold humor, a genius for organization and a dream of empire. He was also an unscrupulous Indian trader, a merciless destroyer of Indians. In *Ponteach*, Rogers seemed to set down episodes from his own ruthless career, yet with bitter satire. Rascally traders set the story in motion. The white governors are Sharp, Gripe and Catchum; the commanders of the fort are Cockum and Frisk. All these people lie, cheat, fill the Indians with cheap rum, and are so short-sighted, so greedily concerned with the wealth of the forest—fur— that they plunge themselves as well as the Indians into disaster. Ponteach, on the other hand, is a noble figure: he was the Ottawa chief who figured largely in the French and Indian War. Rogers had known Ponteach at Detroit when he led his rangers there at the end of the campaign, and, though the nobility of the chief's character has been questioned by a few contemporary historians, on the whole the portrait in the play has been accepted pretty much as Rogers drew it. Parkman and others have followed its outline.

Why Rogers lampooned his own character and exploits in the play is an enigma that will probably remain insoluble. He is said to have written it during a brief visit to London in 1776, and his authorship has been denied, though without the indication of another source. From his stories, his journals, from a few copies of the treaties a literary carpenter might have put the play together, turning the tables on Rogers by its satire; but he is usually accepted as the author, and the play established a dramatic pattern that was long to endure, that was clearly our own. Strange as was the satire on the white men in *Ponteach*, this was only part of a whole reversal of attitudes which might have been expected. As the title signifies, the Ottawa chief is the hero; his character is exalted. The interaction between the whites and the Indians was precisely that often sketched by the Indians in the treaties in protest. The Indians had somehow imposed their own view on this first imaginative embodiment of the two races. The noble savage emerged; and strangely enough this concept fitted a body of philosophical thought emerging in Europe. This was the concept long since embedded in Montaigne's little essay on "Cannibals." It had been abstractly assumed by Vico and had been powerfully outlined by Rousseau in the *Discours* some fifteen years before *Ponteach* appeared. The frontiersman Rogers would hardly have read any of these works, either in London or New England, though there is some evidence that the *Discours* reached Salem, at least, not long after its publication. In any event this concept was materialized at full length in the play, probably for the first time, certainly for the first time in the new world. In it were embodied not only the concept of the noble savage—the child of nature—but also Rousseau's ideas as to the damaging effect of civilization, in portrayal of the white trappers, traders and officers. None of this was in philosophical terms, but the meaning was unmistakable.

This effort at perspective and judgment was a bold achievement when relationships between the Indians and the whites were still unresolved and even bitter. Something headlong appears in it, and the resulting portraiture of the Indians belonged to fantasy: it was an ideal, another eidolon. But the mood which was to be sustained in many similar portrayals was wholly different from that with which the Yankee had been drawn or the sketchy backwoodsman and Negro. The American self-portraits— as in a genuine sense they were—showed a shrewd realism, a pawky humor, an entire lack of flattery or illusion. Ponteach was drawn almost tenderly, without any attempt at realism—even the lively touches with which the Indian chiefs often embellished references to themselves in the treaties were missing. The underlying American attitude was persistent, surviving the clash of events, the lapse of years, accompanying downright warfare with the Indians.

In 1774, the Mingo chief Logan, who had long considered himself a friend of the whites, found his family slaughtered in the Yellow Creek Massacre. His bitterness was unbounded. Later he sent a terse communication to Lord Dunmore through whom it was published in the *Virginia Gazette*. It "flew," as Jefferson said, "through all the papers of the continent and through the magazines and other publications of Great Britain: and those who were boys at that time will attest that the speech of Logan used to be given them as a school exercise for repetition." Young American orators were indeed to practice and rehearse its inflections for years, with the tragic climax: "This called on me for revenge. I have sought it. I have killed many, I have fully glutted my vengeance. For my country I rejoice at the beams of peace. But do not harbor the thought that mine is the joy of fear. Logan never felt fear. He will not turn his heel to save his life. Who is there to mourn for Logan? Not one."

Jefferson's inclusion of the speech in his *Notes on Virginia* gave rise to the theory that he was its author, but he had only offered it as testimony in what had become a *cause célèbre*, that created by Raynal's remarks on the degeneration of natural life in America. The speech was offered as proof to the contrary, for its noble qualities. He explicitly denied that he had written it, but he undoubtedly extended its currency. Some seventy years after it was sent to Lord Dunmore, the speech was enshrined by McGuffey in his Fifth Reader, again with the declaration that Jefferson had written it. As a boy of Shadwell, Jefferson had listened to the oratory of the great Cherokee warrior Ontassere: his knowledge of the Indian manner of address and of Indian ceremonials was ample. Few themes were more frequently touched upon in his writings than Indian customs, history, wars, language, treaties, councils, government. No doubt he could have written such a speech as that of Logan, but his participation in the imaginative tradition of the tribes was far broader and more significant. As President he continued the great cycle of the treaties, speaking for the government where in earlier periods diverse groups of white men had spoken for the colonies, and preserving in perfection the ancient rituals, the established symbols, the broad dramatic form. Today Jefferson's Indian addresses are far too little known; but with the Indian replies and the climactic treaties they too merge into the history of the American drama.

In their own time these treaties and the circumstances that surround them were widely known. When the Seneca chiefs came to Washington for their conferences, their portraits were drawn in noble profile by the French artist St. Memin, whose work in this manner was having a widespread vogue. The spirit was clearly that of commemoration: with all the ceremonial gravity, the outcome for the great tribes was tragic retreat. A few individuals such as the Moravian missionaries Heckewelder and Zeisberger were seeking to frame a mode of existence between the two races, and Jefferson had this purpose in view, but the elegiac mood prevailed. Freneau's verses on Indian themes were in this vein. In *The Contrast*, Tyler somewhat irrelevantly introduced a Cherokee lament, which he may or may not have written: this plaintive song of Indian submission to fate had an enormous vogue, was printed as a broadside, found its way into the songsters, and had an independent existence down the century in many an out-of-the-way village.

All the arts were engaged by this theme, but its widest expression was to be found in the drama or the theater. Beginning with *Ponteach*, the effort to portray the Indian character in flowery idealized fashion was consistent, emerging in the broad historical pantomimes that so engaged the American fancy in the years immediately following the Revolution. In *Tammany* the theme went off into boisterous masquerade, but this only proved it to be so familiar that it could be played with. In one fashion the whites had often masqueraded as Indians. That stirring pageant known as the Boston Tea Party, with New England citizens expressing their instinct for theater and drama as well as their rebellion, had been an instance: it may well be a question whether the participants enjoyed more dumping the tea in the harbor or masquerading in warpaint and feathers with brandished tomahawks. On every frontier the whites had adopted Indian dress, had used Indian weapons, had quickly learned to scalp their enemies, indeed often scalped the Indians to obtain bounties. Even as *Tammany* was being produced in New York, it was being noted regretfully in the New England village of Marietta on the Ohio that some young men had come back from a foray into the wilderness with the scalp of only one Indian.

Paradoxically, even as these Indian themes were being

developed on the stage and elsewhere, savagery between the two races was reaching a new intensity. The Battle of Fallen Timbers on the Maumee in 1794 had seemed a decisive defeat for the Indians in the newly expanding West; but their struggle continued underground. Tecumseh and his twin brother Tenskwatawa—sometimes called Elkswatawa—of the Shawnees became engaged in a far-reaching conspiracy that was political, intellectual, legalistic, religious, even philosophical. By shrewd reasoning Tecumseh argued that the Indian treaties relating to the Ohio country should be declared void, since the undoubted fact of Indian communal ownership had not been recognized in their formulation. By no means all the tribes sharing the Indian lands had given their consent to the transfer. Tecumseh, who must be ranked as a statesman, was a powerful orator. He was no less effective in quiet counsels around the fire at night; he moved, a tireless shadow, from tribe to tribe over wide reaches of the western territory. Tenskwatawa was able to stir in his listeners a mystic sense of unity, the remembrance of ancient loyalties: he possessed and practiced the gifts of the revivalist. The two brothers became engaged in the clash of empire as had the earlier tribes: now rather than the French it was the British who seemed a source of strength. Tecumseh was encouraged to believe that an Indian buffer state might be created in the West which would restore to the tribes their ancient lands, their dignity, their power. Harrison, recognizing Tecumseh's genius for leadership, maneuvered his brother into defeat at Tippecanoe. Tecumseh fell at the Battle of the Thames. Their vast program had carried them into the War of 1812. Tenskwatawa, broken in power, moved west, across the Mississippi. But the struggle was not over. The Creeks, who had been pushed from their hunting grounds in Tennessee, had joined with the British to the south. Jackson's treaty-making with the defeated Creeks had a barbaric splendor. The chieftains were received with the customary dignity, but the outcome was familiar. This was the last of the great ceremonial treaties, though others retained the framework of the past. In spite of the fact that the tribes were considered nations treating in equality with the United states, in spite of earnest diplomatic assurances, pressure upon the tribes continued. Their lands were continually being seized on flimsy pretexts by speculators. They were soon to begin their exodus into the West along what they called "the trail of tears."

It was during the period between the two wars for national independence that the Indian was fully enshrined on the stage with outlines that were to endure, as if the triumphant ghost of the race imposed itself upon the conquerors in spite of the continued struggle and defeat. The drawing continued to be bold, tender, elegiac; the mournful backward glance was persistent. The story of Pocahontas and John Smith was told with music in an "operatic melodrama," *The Indian Princess*, by J. N. Barker, which became vastly popular, and was one of the first

American plays to be produced in London. The Pocahontas story was to be repeated again and again. For a
brief time these portrayals of the Indian on the stage
ceased after the War of 1812, as if the fantasy had been
shattered, but they were resumed at least by 1823 with
a play based on the life of Logan. The stream of Indian
plays had again begun in earnest, some of them having
to do with Washington's journey to the Ohio country before the Revolution. The Pocahontas story took on a fresh
existence. By this time Cooper had written *The Last of
the Mohicans.* The Indian theme was prominent in both
the novel and the play in the immediately ensuing years,
but it may be noted that this theme had first arisen
broadly in the drama and the theater or in related forms
and was sustained in these before it was taken over in
the more discursive writing of the novel. The direct
graphic display of the theater seemed instinctively chosen
by the new Americans as their own rather than the
slower, sometimes richer approaches of the long narrative.

These Indian plays were naive, even primitive, they
had an engaging simplicity of outline, but they were
cleaving out salient American preoccupations within the
popular forum of the theater. The persistence of the
theme may be construed as representing a troubled col-
lective conscience, an effort to obliterate a wrong by
handsome tributes. In some measure it seemed a part of
the wish to establish a past which so comically—as Irving

noted in another connection in his preface to the *Knicker-bocker History*—often went back to the dawn of civiliza-tion. Yet it was clearly related to the philosophical idea first fully formulated by Rousseau, the persuasive concept of "the child of nature," the related idea that nature was good. Suggested by *Ponteach,* this underlying idea was continued in a patriotic play of 1776, *The Fall of British Tyranny,* in which Tammany with other Indians were briefly sketched, to music. From his throne in "the crotch of a tree," Tammany dispensed justice and insisted upon liberty, expressing a philosophy close to that of Rousseau—

> In freedom's bright cause Tammany pled with applause
> And reasoned most justly from nature.

In his preface to *The Indian Princess,* Barker alludes to Rousseau. Sentiment was undoubtedly interwoven with this philosophical idea as was a sheer liking for the under-lying stories. Nowhere in the Indian plays was nature apprehended as the Indian had apprehended it, with a deep animism, with lovely trenchant metaphors, yet the new Americans had sought to keep something of this poetry when they retained many of the Indian place-names, beautiful in sound and suggestion.

The names of Indian villages were often kept, even when the original inhabitants had been ruthlessly ex-pelled. Nature in the plays was airy and flowery and re-mote. Hardly a touch of the earthy American landscape

appeared there. Nature was drawn as the Indian characters were drawn, as fantasy, as belonging to the realm of
untethered ideas. A kind of lilt ran through the plays
even when their outcome was tragic: they were light,
even a little merry, and the tragedy rarely ran deep.

The Indian plays remained the means by which this
philosophy of nature was most clearly expressed on the
stage, yet it was by no means confined to them, but found
expression in such plays as *The Child of Feeling* and
Nature and Philosophy, and infused a new exaltation of
rural life in *The Forest Rose,* an opera first produced in
1825 and a perennial success, in which the philosophy of
nature was somehow flung around the spare figure of
Yankee Jonathan. The Yankee—and perhaps more generally the American—seemed to be reaching the conclusion
that he too was "a child of nature." Irony may be discovered in the fact that these ideas were first materialized in
a play that came out of New England, *Ponteach,* and that
they were being repeated in relation to the Yankee character.

II. SUSANNAH ROWSON

Pocahontas was usually given a touch of gentility in
the Indian plays, something silky and glossy. Gentility
might be discovered in the music and the words of *The
Forest Rose* and elsewhere in pretty little operatic ballads.
Gentility has been considered as having exerted its desic-

cating influence in this period, a forerunner of a wider destructive movement to come in later years. Certainly the insidious element appeared, the spread of a would-be elegance; but it was by no means new. Godfrey, who wrote *The Prince of Parthia,* was only one of many *littérateurs* of the colonial era who practiced the turning of verses, the writing of smooth little essays. Yet gentility had its other phases; it was by no means always quite genteel, as is shown by the vigorous career of Susannah Rowson, actress, playwright and novelist. Graphic display was an art in which Mrs. Rowson was adept: her life and her character upset a number of plausible theories, among them that which assigns to woman in this era a minor, submissive position. Truly enough the main figures of the stage were masculine—not only the actors but the parts were male; the great patriot heroes were men; the Yankee, the other lesser American types, the Indians of the stage, with the exception of Pocahontas, were all men. This vigorous world seemed wholly masculine. Mrs. Rowson arises to prove the contrary in more than one direction, and she dispels the notion that gentility in this period was a negative quality. It was resilient, its fabric was strong, even tough.

Mrs. Rowson was never languid. Something big and bosomy might be discovered in her most sentimental fiction; her energy was unbounded. When she found herself without money in London after an unfortunate marriage and a round of novel-writing that had yielded her little remuneration, she decided to go on the stage, though she was untrained for it. As an admirer said, she "had a face beaming with expression, an easy and polite manner, a retentive memory," all desirable, he thought, for an actress. He might have added that she had an incisive profile, revealing other qualities of measurable assistance in a career. Mrs. Rowson never lacked determination or initiative. She played her parts with some liveliness for a year and then was engaged by Wignell, who had come from Philadelphia to augment the company for his new Chestnut Street Theatre, and who no doubt saw an honest advantage in the fact that she was the author of *Charlotte Temple*, which had made her famous on both sides of the Atlantic.

Though Mrs. Rowson was born in England, she must be counted as an American because her subsequent career and most of her youth were spent in this country. Her father, Lieutenant Haswell, a revenue officer in the service of the Crown, had brought his family to Nantasket in 1762 when Susannah was aged four. The hard wintry voyage ended in shipwreck one dark night. At dawn little Susannah was swung by a rope over a perilous sea into the arms of a sailor; and this was only the beginning of her complex adventures. A number of well-to-do Boston families came to Nantasket for the summer, among them that stormy, unflinching patriot, James Otis, who seems to have found her a bright child: while she was still of a tender age they carried on literary conversations. From Otis she may have gained something akin to her later

passionate faith in the cause of the Republic, and, since
the stay of the Rowsons at Nantasket was a long one, she
may even have had some knowledge of the plays written
in behalf of the Revolutionary cause by James Otis's sister, Mercy Warren. But when the war broke out her family remained loyalist; they were isolated by the patriot
forces and suffered destitution.

When at last they returned to London, Susannah was
a young lady and her life seemed to reach a dead level.
She became a governess and finally married Mr. Rowson
"by the persuasion of her friends," as was afterwards explained: but if this venture seemed colorless and passive,
actually its sequences betrayed a considerable initiative
on the part of Mrs. Rowson. Her husband became a shadowy figure, though he never quite vanished. When Mrs.
Rowson embarked upon a stage career, Mr. Rowson likewise became an actor. When she left it, he left. He was
unfaithful, he even had a natural child, yet he remained
on the scene and was referred to as part of Mrs. Rowson's
establishment toward the end of her fairly long life. And
she educated the natural child, which was surely not
quite genteel.

Yet a surface gentility belonged to her career as a
writer in London: she had entered upon it entirely for
pecuniary reasons, but she managed to convey the idea
that for her writing was only a pleasurable accomplishment. She was one of those women who are said to have
a gifted pen, which somehow removes them from the

coarse realm of effort. "What," said a Grub Street journalist upon meeting the dainty heroine of her *Mentoria*, undoubtedly herself, "can that young creature be an author?" But she brightly satirized this hack writer with his scissors and paste. She worked hard at her trade, and wrote one sentimental novel after another in an easy style that must have cost her some effort, none of them without some touch of originality, all of them with a distinct bias. Already Mrs. Rowson was a reformer: her novels rarely contained an irresistible story, but they always had a purpose. They also had an underlying bias. They were feminist. Mrs. Rowson looked upon the male sex with a skeptical eye. In her *Victoria*, the heroine loses her mind as a result of male scheming; indeed her delicate, distraught heroines almost invariably suffered deeply through masculine faults, failures or downright deviltry. In *Charlotte Temple*, seduction was the single primary theme upon which she harped. Written in liquid prose, pervaded by verses and songs into which the unhappy heroine slipped as easily as she slipped to her downfall, the novel was based upon facts which Mrs. Rowson took no pains to disguise. Indeed she flaunted them. Mr. Rowson's dereliction does not seem to have been directly exposed though it probably gave her momentum. The "fiendish libertine" was called Montresor, which was the middle name of one of Mrs. Rowson's stepbrothers, who was still alive at the time the novel was published. Poor Charlotte seems to have been a real person: her ashes are supposed to rest in Trinity Churchyard in New York. Perhaps a knowledge of these circumstances gave the novel its first great vogue in England and the United States, but only its driving energy of style could have kept it alive—and alive it is to this day. Long and plotless as her other novels are, they had motion and purpose, but none of them, not even the sequel *Charlotte's Daughter,* which trenched upon the fearful theme of incest, had the success of *Charlotte.*

Mrs. Rowson failed to guard her own interests in this novel, and she was making only a precarious living when Wignell saw her in London. Her acting was never notable; her main accomplishment in the theater consisted of her plays, which by no means followed the pattern of her novels. Her feminism remained intact, but she soared straight out of a morbid preoccupation with seduction and incest into the high air of patriotism. She flung herself headlong into a phase of the theater that was ardently given to patriotic themes, but she gave them a broadly feminist bias of her own, which in spite of arch phrases and the silky surface she knew so well how to contrive was anything but genteel; and she accomplished these purposes with a great fanfare.

Nothing less than the popular operatic form would do for her first play, *Slaves of Algiers.* One of the best-known composers of the day, Reinagle, composed the music. Mrs. Rowson created a neat part for herself as one of the captured American women, and for the epilogue she con-

trived a playful little scene into which she was rushed by
the prompter before the final curtain. Fluttering, she ex-
plains she's

> in such a flurry
> Do let me stop a moment! just for breath,
> Bless me! I'm almost terrified to death,
> Yet sure, I had no real cause for fear,
> Since none but liberal—generous friends are here.
> Say, will you kindly overlook my errors?
> You smile—then to the winds I give my terrors.

But into these coy lines she worked a statement of her
theme, that women "should have supreme dominion," and
she meant it. The whole play revolved about women; they
dominated the plot, the action, the outcome. Moreover,
the play had an assertive rollicking note, which was
quickly perceived by William Cobbett, who heartily disliked the play and lampooned it coarsely in a pamphlet
called *A Kick for a Bite*. In reply she alluded to Cobbett
as "a loathsome kind of reptile," a judgment in which
many Americans of the time concurred. By way of the
stage, Mrs. Rowson had plunged into the thick of affairs
with a certain journalistic timeliness. Mary Wollstonecraft's *A Vindication of the Rights of Women* was published in Philadelphia at about the time Mrs. Rowson's
play was produced, and was followed three years later by
Alcuin, A Dialogue on the Rights of Women by Charles
Brockden Brown, the disciple of Godwin, a friend of the
actor Cooper. Moreover, Mrs. Rowson was one of the

first to make the treatment of Americans by Algerian pirates in the Mediterranean a patriotic cause. She anticipated Royall Tyler's novel on this theme by several years. She might almost be said, in regard to this vexing situation, to have lighted the patriotic torch.

Cobbett might storm: her play was immensely popular. Undaunted by the controversy, apparently enjoying it, she dashed off a musical farce, *The Volunteers*, using a political theme that to some ladies would have seemed unsuitable, the Whiskey Rebellion. On the heels of this came her *Female Patriot*, in which she played on all the strings. After she left the stage in 1797, she had one more fling at play-writing in her *Columbia's Daughters*, whose feminism was resonant.

Boston might have seemed the last place in the United States where an actress could find an accepted place—an actress who had handled seduction and politics in no uncertain terms and had launched forth in a radical feminism as well. But when a company in which she was playing dissolved in Boston, Mrs. Rowson glided, apparently without an effort, into a recognized position there. Boston seemed unperturbed by these activities, nor in essentials did she subdue them. She merely gave them a different form. She established a school for well-born young ladies in which she utilized many of the modes and materials belonging to the stage. Nor was her position in any way subservient. Whatever the position of the child's parents, she never hesitated to write "incorrigible" on a report card. She was never prim, quite the contrary. She played the guitar for her pupils, sang them merry ballads, led them through the lively steps of the contra-dance. Never afraid of innovation, she substituted the piano for the ancient harpsichord in her school and employed as a teacher Gottlieb Graupner, recently arrived from Hanover, who was to exercise a strong influence upon the rapidly expanding musical life in Boston.

Gentility abounded in Mrs. Rowson's educational efforts, but it was a gentility with freshness and stamina. If her young ladies painted fruit, flowers and landscapes, if they embroidered elaborately on satin, their talents and their handiwork really bloomed. Nor did she confine them to the more obviously polite feminine accomplishments. Precisely for their use she compiled a collection of rhymes and dialogues called *A Present for Young Ladies,* to train them in a dramatic art, that of public declamation. Noah Webster was employing such dialogues in his new readers; collections of dialogues, plays and declamations were beginning to appear in numbers for the training of youth in public speech. These publications belonged to a great wave of popular taste, effort, energy. Oratory, so closely linked with the arts of the stage, was becoming one of the great American arts. The orators of the Revolution had gone: a new school was arising in which young Daniel Webster, John C. Calhoun and Henry Clay in Kentucky were already conspicuous figures. Their arts of speech were wholly those of the stage. On the other hand, the stage had adopted politics: the political orators and the people of the stage seemed to mingle their special vocations. On the stage itself declamation often was to be heard as a distinct feature. Thomas Cooper would recite *Alexander's Feast* with unparalleled dramatic effect between the major drama and the afterpiece, and declamations, similar in purpose if not in effect, were common on the programs of the many Thespian societies now being formed in remote Western villages. Political oratory was showing a new vigor.

What was novel, what was fearlessly Mrs. Rowson's own was the training of young women in the art of public speech, yet it must be noted that in this innovation she was by no means pushing upstream in Boston. Mary Wollstonecraft was being read there as elsewhere. Still further, a number of young Boston women had made a radical experiment based upon their reading of Locke's essay, *Some Thoughts Concerning Education.* They had let their girls as well as their boys go barefoot in winter, to harden them, according to what were believed to be the precepts of nature. Royall Tyler's young wife was to remember this adventure in natural philosophy, pedagogy and incipient feminism in some detail. Down the years we may see the figure of a young woman arising from this whole nexus of ideas: Margaret Fuller, born on the edge of Boston in 1810, whose feminist writings with their philosophical bias seemed in the direct line, whose "Con-

versations" fell in with the practice of public dialogues
for women.

Nothing suggested that Mrs. Rowson's feminist bias
was regarded as singular in Boston. Her somewhat boisterous play, *Columbia's Daughters,* was written after her
academy was established, and was performed at least
in New York. She wrote a poem on "The Rights of
Women"—

> While patriots on wide philosophic plan
> Declaim upon the wondrous rights of man.

If the verses were rough the equalitarian idea was ex-
pounded with firmness. Her song, "America, Commerce,
and Freedom," was called "certainly too boisterous for the
pen of a lady" by one of her admirers of much later years
who had never known her; he called it "masculine." It
was, in fact, a drinking song which roughly called money
"the chink." It included lines about tossing off a glass to
a favorite lass, and even urged each bonny lass for her
own part to toss off a glass. Intended to promote a belief
in American maritime power, this piece clearly sprang
from a genuine patriotic sentiment. Curiously enough, it
also derived from Mrs. Rowson's own experience at sea.
At some time in her varied life she seems to have learned
how to navigate a ship. Where? Under what circumstances? We have only the meager, tantalizing fact; but
we may be sure that any ship she steered bounded with
precision over the billows. She accomplished her purpose

in the song—indeed more than she can have hoped for. "America, Commerce, and Freedom" became enormously popular. It was printed as a broadside and in many songsters and was noisily sung in taverns and other popular places for at least twenty-five years. Nor did its light-hearted verses or its popularity or the fact that it was a drinking song damage Mrs. Rowson's position in Boston. When her *Miscellaneous Poems* was published in 1804, a handsome list of well-known Bostonians was announced as subscribers. It may be recalled that during all this period both Mr. Rowson and the natural child were on the scene.

With her ample versatility, Mrs. Rowson managed to engage in a considerable number of literary activities while maintaining her school, which steadily prospered. She wrote for and helped to edit *The Gleaner*, in which a number of plays were published, and in 1802 she became editor of the *Boston Weekly Magazine*. At the same time she wrote a large amount of verse, much of it related to the drama: the declamatory ode was one of her favorite forms. Her "Child of Mortality" was set to music by John Bray and sung with great effect by the newly established Handel and Haydn Society, as was her long ambitious ode entitled "Charity." The great vogue of the oratorio—so close to spoken eloquence—was well under way in Boston as elsewhere, and with her usual responsive fluency Mrs. Rowson had approached this broad form.

Neatness as distinguished from the billowing touch of

her plays belonged to these efforts; even her drinking song might be called neat. She was not truly a poet, but she carved a niche for herself among those American verse-makers who were long to be called poets, and she was better than many of them. She was not truly a dramatist, an actress, a novelist, nor in the full sense an educator, but in each of these roles she had managed to give momentum to broad tendencies. Mrs. Rowson died in 1824. On the walls of Boston houses in which she was surely welcome were portraits of women of a somewhat older generation to whom she must have felt akin. A few of them, like Mrs. Sylvanus Bourne, whom Copley had painted, still lingered, now very old. Elegant in their stiff silks, fine mulls, pearls, elaborate headdresses, they might seem concerned only with such matters, yet clearly enough they were women of principles and ideas. Shrewd, tolerant, hardy, they belonged to a provincial society but exceeded it: in a genuine sense, with their own particular bias, they were women of the great world. They would have understood Mrs. Rowson. They would have admired the strict fashion in which she had tethered a buoyant temperament to a prolonged series of tasks. They were advocates of discipline. But they also would have relished the ebullience running so engagingly through her character, for they had *esprit,* they had belonged to the Revolution.

III. AFTER THE REVOLUTION

With the close of the Revolution, the theater had begun
to flourish, though often in the form of pageantry. At the
end of 1783, Charles Willson Peale was working hurriedly
on a triumphal arch for the public celebration of the
treaty of peace soon to be ratified in Philadelphia. Its
symbolism was riotous. Not a niche, not a panel, not a
flat space was left without an emblem. Branches of fruit,
the lilies of France, the thirteen stars, a parade of militia,
portraits of notables, Moravians building a church for the
Indians, a magnificent figure of Washington as Cincin-
natus resigning his sword for the plow were portrayed
on the frame and canvas structure, while high above in
the center arose the figure of Peace, which at the proper
moment was to be illuminated, casting a glow downward
upon the assembled throng below. For this effect more
than a thousand candles were to be lighted and at the
same time a great burst of rockets was to suffuse the sky
with brilliance.

The celebration took place on the evening of January
22, 1784. Alas, a stray rocket set fire to the flimsy arch
and it went up in a quick blaze and Peale was badly
burned. No one seemed to regard the fiasco as a symbol,
least of all the restless, inventive artist. He quickly began
work on a new arch at Annapolis upon which he lavished

three months' labor, and this was shown in all its symbolic glory at the Proclamation of the final treaty signed there in May.

Already known for his portraits of Washington, painted in camp during the Revolution, Peale was to create a great series of transparencies showing Washington and other national heroes, or national triumphs on sea or land which were carried through streets or shown in large lighted windows. By means of gauzes, puppetry, shifting lights and shadows, he also contrived something resembling a motion picture—perhaps our first—portraying the triumphant engagement of John Paul Jones. Fetes and outdoor spectacles abounded at this time. Washington seldom traveled without passing through classic arches to the accompaniment of music composed for the occasion. Laurel wreaths were dropped upon his brow, one of these arriving in this position through the use of an ingenious mechanism invented by Peale. Almost any play might be turned into a spectacle. William Dunlap's *André,* a thoughtful drama in blank verse, started off in this measured form, with Washington at the opening watching his own portrayal with intense absorption; but once the ceremonial first performances were over, many scenes and the psychological problems involved in the action were dropped and the piece was blown up into a spectacle called *The Glory of Columbia,* with a broad scattering of songs. The launching of the ship *Constitution* was celebrated by a topical sketch with marine background scenery bordering on the marvelous, with a final climactic picture of Niagara Falls.

Franklin's memory was kept green by a spectacle play, *Americana and Elutheria; or a New Tale of the Genii*, through whose flamboyance wandered a purely political theme. A "masque" was produced against a vast scenic background, a cloudy peak high in the Alleghenies, with resounding speeches in blank verse and pantomime by a bevy of nymphs—Horbla, Damonello, Lucifero, Horrendum, Luciabello, Tinteretto, Juberia—who represented all shades of good and evil emotion. The action came to a climax when Tyranny and Pride triumphed over Liberty, who fell into a death-like sleep; whereupon France came on the scene with Fulmenifer, none other than Franklin, who emerged from stormy black clouds amid a display of forked lightning with a lightning-rod in his hand. This he courteously handed to France, who pointed it at Tyranny and Pride. The electric fluid played brightly, they fell transfixed, and Liberty was revived by the application of science. Her prostrate body was carried toward the two evil spirits until her feet touched theirs. Electricity flowed from their galvanized forms and restored her to animation. Bounding up, she joined America in a deep embrace, which included Franklin and France, and the spacious finale showed the emotional nymphs spread out in tableaux on the mountain peak, a bit of patriotic bravura, for the Alleghenies had become a symbol of the sweep of national power on this continent.

Two years before in Charleston a pantomime of the same order had been produced whose major theme was Franklin, *The Apotheosis of Franklin, or His Reception in the Elysian Field*, with many scenes, new decorations, dresses, music, all for the "glorie, energie, and virtue" of Franklin.

Franklin's death seemed to generate an exultant sense of national possession rather than a consciousness of loss. Symbolism was rife in all this pageantry: national events were translated into its forms and floated on music, in the midst of splendid scenery. *The Fourth of July, or the Temple of American Independence*, produced in New York in 1799 with music by Belissier, showed a view of the lower part of Broadway, the Battery, the harbor, and shipping, all painted "on the spot." A military procession appeared in the distance, and in the end the spectators were permitted an inside view of the Temple. The Battle of Trenton formed the spectacular theme of a similar piece, and, if *Arthur and Emmeline* had originally belonged to Dryden, it belonged to the American public by the time the managers produced it. Perhaps they expected it to belong to the ages. It traced the story of civilization from the mythical era of Woden, Thor and Frigga, to the time of Merlin, who by enchantment displayed to King Arthur the whole progress of the American nation from its infancy to its new power. Indians in canoes were shown in the American wilderness and the arrival of Columbus. From then on nothing seems to have been omitted down to the rout of the British; and in fact, after Washington's march and a grand finale in which the glories of the American Navy were brought into view, Merlin looked into the future and indicated triumphs which were to follow in all fields for the new nation.

The Charleston audience before which the Franklin "masque" was first performed—*Americana and Elutheria,* 1798—clearly understood its implications. Written during the Revolution with grateful remembrances of France, it revived those remembrances to answer the Federalists' cry of "Jacobin" and their insistent disparagement of France. Ancestral ties among the people of Charleston were strong. Though they did not accept the extremes of the French Revolution, they saw clearly enough the partisan fashion in which the attack was being used. Their main bias was Jeffersonian, and when the play was published several years later it was dedicated to Jefferson.

A considerable amount of cold water was thrown upon playwrights and managers of the anti-Federalist persuasion a few months after the performance of this piece by the passage of the Alien and Sedition Acts, so stringent was their application in matters of political controversy, so involved with affairs relating to France. The effect of these on the theater was unmistakable. Indeed in the year 1799 no plays whatever by Americans seem to have been published. But the repeal of the acts after the election of Jefferson released political energies that again flowed into drama, and in the *Essex Junto* monarchical

plans attributed to Adams were roundly satirized. Adams
was portrayed as the Duke of Braintree, Hamilton somewhat unhandsomely as General Creole, the thin somber
Pickering as the Earl of Indigo. The play took on added
sharpness because it was published under the long nose
of Pickering in Salem, as was a related dramatic sketch,
Jefferson and Liberty. If the "God-provoking Democrats"
thus swung into action with some imagination and ingenuity, the Federalists also used the drama in *The
Politician Outwitted*, a tract for the times in which the
ignoble politician was an anti-Federalist. A group of
heated Federalist sketches stemmed from the Whiskey
Rebellion, which gave an easy handle for "anti-Jacobin"
sentiments. Nor were plays with political themes the only
means of conveying partisan arguments. Sudden improvisations, asides and songs with political references were
folded into many a play whose subject was of quite a
different order. The always elastic *entr'actes* were often
packed with them. Some of these pieces were hardly plays
at all but omnibus inclusions of the latest news, the latest
partisan arguments. Dunlap's *Liberal Opinions* indicates
further the discursive, intellectual turn the drama had
taken.

Not all the plays with political themes were produced;
many of them were only printed, obtaining thus a considerable currency; and they often possessed what in
music is called attack. Whether or not they were bludg-
eoning an individual, a cause or a sum of events, they

plunged headlong into their themes. Nothing seemed too
ambitious for them. The expanse of spectacle was retained on the professional stage with or without excuse
as a response to a lively taste. Managers went bankrupt
attempting to purvey novel scenery and often altered
sober dramas into something hardly recognizable in order
to create scenic effects. On the stage almost any of these
pieces, however serious the political argument, was likely
to run off buoyantly into music—music was everywhere.
Our first opera, *Tammany,* was written to praise the
newly formed Tammany Society of New York, whose intentions were violently anti-Federalist. Produced in three
cities in 1794—New York, Philadelphia, Boston—it stirred
controversies that spilled over into newspapers and no
doubt induced rejoinders in other plays. In *Tammany,*
the spread of a grandiose, spectacular theme was well to
the fore—*Tammany,* or Tamamend, still the patron saint
of the Society, was the Delaware chief who had welcomed
William Penn, according to tradition. Thus the door was
opened for a lavish spectacle showing forests, massed Indians in costume, the oncoming whites. Since the libretto
has not survived, we cannot be sure of the details except
that they were lavish. The readiness with which the book
and the music were to disappear was a sign of the careless ease with which such productions were concocted.

On the whole, the rising Jeffersonians seem to have
been gayer and more musical than the Federalists, for
not only does their print lie upon our first opera but they

achieved another called a "comic opera" a few years later, *Federalism Triumphant,* a splashing, candid, satirical farce set to music.

Music bubbled up on the stage in a fashion that has been called "lyric," as if song were irresistible, but its effects seem to have been less often lyric than choral with chiming dialogue and clashing musical shouts. English ballad-opera received a great impetus from Washington's enjoyment of *The Poor Soldier,* which he saw many times in the years immediately following the Revolution; no doubt his well-known fondness for music as for the theater had a marked effect in obtaining sanction for these diversions after the ban of the Continental Congress. Most of the music for the theater was composed or improvised by English musicians who hastened to these shores after the peace. It was a poor time for them in England, where music was at low ebb; and no doubt they came here filled with the most idealistic expectations of a whole new world. A certain amount of wreckage followed. So insistent was the popular demand for the spectacular, the operatic, the contentious, for novelties, that no composer could write deliberately, finish carefully, or sustain a serious mood. The popular temper might be intellectual as in the political arguments on the stage, but it could hardly be called serious.

A gifted composer, an able dramatist—Benjamin Carr and William Dunlap—collaborated in *The Archers,* a highly original piece based on the life of William Tell which antedated Rossini's opera by thirty years. With its heroic subject, its republican theme, the story seemed particularly well suited to the theater of the young nation, so acutely conscious of having achieved its liberty. But the opera was hastily concocted; serious episodes were transformed into noisy comedy; the music became increasingly brisk as the piece progressed. *The Archers* was quickly transformed into a fairly riotous celebration.

Yet the operatic form was a lively favorite everywhere, with ballets and an orchestra. A high standard of operatic performance was often maintained, at least for brief periods, particularly by Wignell in Philadelphia, Baltimore and Washington. For some five years from 1794, Hartford had summer opera with as many as twenty-four performances in a single season. The music was mainly French and confections like those of Rousseau, Grétry, Pergolesi and Paisiello were offered and well received. Rousseau's effort to take the theater back to nature in his pastoral *Le Devin du Village* appeared more than once on the American stage. French opera with imported musicians and singers was performed in the larger cities up to and even including "the troublesome year" 1798, when anti-Jacobin sentiment was reaching a crest; and indeed between 1793 and 1800 more than a hundred musical dramas were produced in the country. These performances were not always peaceful. Opinion as to the French Revolution clashed openly in the theater with hisses, catcalls, shouts of *Ça Ira*, stanzas of the "Marseillaise" and

"Down with the Jacobins." With the passionate journalism belonging to other aspects of the theater, episodes in the French Revolution were dramatized almost as soon as they occurred. The imprisonment of Lafayette became a favored subject, and though such pieces were mainly plays, they had their own bravura with a certain amount of music that brought them close to the operatic.

French opera had its ups and downs in the Atlantic seaboard cities because of changing relations toward France and the vicissitudes of theatrical managers. Full-blown opera was expensive. But in New Orleans its tradition quickly became continuous. First produced in a tent, then in the open air, next in a makeshift theater, French opera was soon a transcendent attraction in this crowded port, nor were the rich creoles its only patrons. Planters with large holdings along the Mississippi frequently listened to opera, as did traders from the Ohio country who began filtering into Louisiana, slowly at first while passage on the Mississippi was in dispute, later in large numbers. Even riverboatmen, their pockets lined with money after the hard, venturesome trip, were patrons of what quickly became a series of highly ambitious productions. By 1807 the St. Philippe Theatre had been completed at the fabulous cost of a hundred thousand dollars, mainly for opera, and two years later the gambler John Davis built the Orleans, which surpassed it in elegance, embarking upon a long career in which he purveyed French or Italian opera—though knowing nothing of music—and made yearly trips to Paris for new scores, new singers, instrumentalists, ballet dancers and scenery, offering all these with a gambler's lavish hand, with an intuitive genius for the lucky and the popular.

Everywhere speculative enterprise poured into the theater. The spacious Chestnut Street in Philadelphia, built for Wignell and completed in 1793, was modeled on the Royal Theatre at Bath in the classic style from designs by Latrobe, with a finely balanced façade, a charming interior and an apron stage. A stock company of great excellence was to be maintained there for twenty-five years. That inveterate gambler John Jacob Astor bought the Park Theatre in New York because of a steadily mounting popular interest. Patronage was mixed, motley, hearty, often coarse. It was some years before women of the streets in the larger cities were forbidden to flaunt themselves in the boxes. Songs, catcalls, back-talk, noisy rows or even riots surged up frequently in response to partisanship on the stage. Before the Revolution the theater had been a luxury, enjoyed mainly by small groups of the well-to-do in New York, Philadelphia, Annapolis, Williamsburg, Charleston. The drama had been an intimate, almost a private affair. Then the theater had been banned by the Continental Congress because of the distractions it might offer and the political allusions it might adroitly contain, but no sooner was the Revolution over than theatricals sprang up everywhere even before the ban was lifted and promptly became a common possession. A broad cross-section of the American public was crowding into the theater as if long bred to it, choosing the free and lively expressive form for its own.

Here and there opposition to the theater appeared. The formal theater developed somewhat later in Boston than in the other seaboard cities. For the most part opposition arose in new communities where what seemed to be prejudice on the part of religious groups perhaps really stemmed from an intuitive sense that the theater was a free and incalculable agent whose force might disrupt the slow growth toward a desired stability. Yet in Pittsburgh, where the Presbyterian influence was strong, amateur theatricals soon had a place, and strolling players appeared early. In the older communities people of the theater were often warmly welcomed not only for their performances but for their lively additions to social life; far from being ostracized, as common theory has it, actors, managers and playwrights had a genuine place among cultivated groups. When Merry the actor died in Baltimore, John Bernard said that half the population of Maryland walked after his coffin, so greatly was he beloved. Thomas Cooper, handsome, graceful, already a success at Covent Garden, came to this country in 1796 and made a fortune in the theater playing Shakespeare and classic parts in which his invincible habit of improvisation was transcended by his fine voice and many-sided characteristics; his ability as a manager almost equaled his gifts as an actor. Like many an American, he was a great gambler both in and out of the theater; and he had great charm of personal address. He married a New York belle, gambled, as did most of the young blades of her circle, hunted with them, and withal had a great taste for philosophy, which came naturally to him since he had been educated by William Godwin. No doubt he deepened the difficult influence of Godwin upon young Brockden Brown, who was struggling with chaotic purposes in his novels; he knew Brown within the purlieus of the famous Friendly Club, as he also knew Irving, Paulding and others who were formally attempting to found an American literature.

The drama had spread into the other arts. Most of the talent for landscape or *genre* seems to have flowed into scene-painting in the theater; and the quick spread into music was marked. In the same fashion many of the people of the theater had inclusive talents, none more than William Dunlap, who has been called the father of the American stage, whose influence during the decade from 1796 to 1806 was paramount. Neither edged nor sparkling as a temperament, Dunlap was enormously absorptive, fluent, friendly. First a painter—sketching both Washington and Mrs. Washington during the Revolution —he went to London for study under West and was to use his only commonplace talents in this direction as a resource when his theatrical projects fell through. Except for a ruined eye no doubt he would have become an actor, so greatly was he attracted to the stage; instead he be-

came a manager, mainly in New York, and wrote, translated or adapted a prodigious number of plays, some sixty
in all. When he went bankrupt because of his passion for
novelty and a lavish use of painted acts, he set about
painting again as an itinerant limner, finding sitters in the
back country as he could, from door to door. Dunlap was
in and out of the theater for many years, as assistant manager to Cooper at the Park, attempting other ventures.
Again he dipped into painting; he knew most of the artists and writers in New York; he too was a member of the
Friendly Club. He founded a magazine, he wrote a life
of Brockden Brown and, with an invincible passion for
personal detail, wrote, before his career had run out, a
monumental history of the American stage, which still
remains a prime source, and an equally important history
of American art or, as he called it, "the arts of design in
America." In addition, he kept voluminous diaries, recording materials on the American arts which he himself did
not exhaust in these two works, nor have they ever been
fully drawn upon. Finally, with an ingratiating fervor,
Dunlap propounded a large idea: he urged the support
of the theater by the separate states or by the national
government.

Nothing came of this proposal. State or national sub-
sidies hardly seemed to be needed when actors and managers flung themselves so generously into the life of the
theater. Like the musicians, many of them came from
England; they often had notable careers behind them.

Wignell had been a member of Garrick's company. Mrs. Hatton, the actress, who wrote *Tammany*, was a sister of Mrs. Siddons. John Bernard was not only an accomplished comedian, he was a man of the great world. In London he had moved in high Whig circles and had had merry exchanges with Fox and Sheridan at the Beefsteak Club. In this country he knew many of Franklin's friends and could interest Washington and Jefferson by his conversations. It is from Bernard that we have salient comments by all three on the arts; but equally, in his richly packed *Retrospections of America*, could he set down racy fresh portrayals of a Yankee stage-driver or tavern-keeper. With an actor's genius for character, Bernard seemed to enter into the very substance of the American temperament; his volume of reminiscences remains one of our richest social pictures of the time. Yet if the level of his writing is unusually high, his general intention was shared by other actors or managers. Not only Dunlap but Hodgkinson, Durang, Wood and Wemyss were to write personal narratives relating to the stage containing essentials of social portraiture that suggest the breadth of their interests and the extent to which they identified themselves with American life. No strict line can be drawn as to citizenship among these people of the theater; but most of them counted themselves as American even when the larger part of their careers had been spent abroad. Some of them established families here whose younger members were to join in the building of American theatrical traditions in later years, the Booths, the Chapmans, the Ostinellis, the Jeffersons, the Placides, with here and there a theatrical family whose lineage was to continue in the other arts. David Poe was one of the many young Americans now being drawn to the stage; his wife Elizabeth came from a family of English actors, her stepfather had set up a theater in Portland. Edgar Allan Poe was born in Boston while his parents were in the midst of a checkered engagement there, in 1809, and two plays in which they had parts curiously forecast his preoccupations as a poet and a story-teller, the cabalistic *Wood Daemon*, the eerie *Castle Spectre*. John Darley, the English comedian, and his wife, who was an actress, came here about 1800 and brought up a young family whose members were to have a place in American portraiture, light music and comic illustration.

Episodes relating to many of these people of the theater were set down by one or another eager critic or historian. Here and there glimpses of personal character shine through, and dozens of acute personal dramas developed, such as those between the Hallams and the Hodgkinsons or within the struggling, buoyant career of Dunlap. Yet nothing like a full personal history of these actors remains. With few exceptions their lives at a distance have the ephemeral character of many of their productions. What remains rather is the stirring effect of their advent upon the American scene. Versatile, talented, they possessed the utopian enthusiasm, the usual daring of people of the theater faced with new countries and new frontiers. They streamed through American life like a broad many-colored ribbon.

Not all the plays produced on their wide circuits up and down the seaboard and into the West were of American origin. Shakespeare was a perennial favorite, particularly the historical tragedies. *Hamlet* was played for the murder, the ghost, the burial; *Macbeth* for the witches, the sleep-walking scene, the knocking at the gate. The more violent scenes from Shakespeare were perennial favorites. *Richard III*, cut to the bone, created a heavy sense of fate. Scale was everywhere in this new theater—scale and violence, in such favorite pieces as *Pizarro, The Iron Chest, Venice Preserved,* as if the violence that had been basic and was still dominant in American frontier experience were transmuted and expressed by these remote situations and alien characters. Dunlap adapted innumerable French and German plays, simplifying them, adding bold new stresses. Managers and playwrights sought materials in a catch-as-catch-can fashion where they could find them in any foreign sources, infusing into them large effects and bold emotions. Strewn over the stage with a free hand, many of these plays lasted only a few nights; others would follow in swift succession as if spectacular change in itself were a prime objective.

So large a number of importations might have been expected to impede the homespun effort, but this seems to have been continuous. Not only managers, musicians, and actors had a hand in creating new plays on American soil, often with native themes, but amateurs from all walks of life wrote plays, lawyers, physicians, a senator, the Librarian of Congress. A great many plays were published anonymously; plays frequently appeared in magazines. Some were circulated and have survived only in manuscript. Not every ambitious young playwright had the delirious experience of a young man who submitted a particularly long heavy tragedy to Hodgkinson, around whom the principal part had been written. Hodgkinson stuffed the manuscript into the pocket of his coat when he went off to hunt in the forests of Brooklyn. Game was plentiful and he presently found himself out of wadding for his gun. Scanning the pages of the play, choosing those that contained his own parts, he tore out pieces, rammed his gun, and, as the hunting remained excellent, the play survived only with great gaps when he returned in the evening to New York. However, Hodgkinson decided to produce it. At the final curtain, the applause was tremendous, but the author bounded out of a box, over the orchestra, across the stage, and into Hodgkinson's dressing-room like a tiger, ready to take the actor by the throat. Hodgkinson retreated with grace, suavely declaring that at least the play had been performed, even though many of the lines had been, so to speak, improvised; and this, as they both well knew, was a great stroke of luck for the young playwright when so many writers were besieging managers and actors merely to glance at their manuscripts.

Topical plays were written with incredible promptness. The quick scaffolding of a play could be run up and the piece acted on the heels of almost any event. Most of these plays were written and produced far too rapidly to permit a sensitive or finished drawing of character. Any preoccupation with individual destiny was missing. Tragedy in a deep sense was not achieved by American playwrights—for the most part the tragedies came from other lands and were likely to take on new stresses in American production, to be offset by riotous afterpieces. Love or passion was never a major theme, not even sentiment in the wide sense. In its marked departure from a concern with individual character, the stage even managed to avoid some of the emotional excesses that were overspreading tales or novels in this period. Sentimentalism had no marked triumphs on the stage; that great subject of the sentimental school, seduction, hardly appeared there at all. In the *Massachusetts Magazine* for 1799, nine out of eleven stories dealt with seduction, and Mrs. Rowson's *Charlotte Temple,* that simple song on this theme, was having a whirlwind popularity that was to continue for decades. The dramatized version of the novel failed; even Mrs. Rowson's popularity as an actress and a dramatist could not give it a vogue. Nor can this marked refusal of the theater have been due to delicate feeling, for its allusions or asides were often rough or rude or sly.

Not a single play of American origin written in this period has the concentration or poetic insight that would have given it enduring worth. Here and there a fine passage in blank verse may be found, a bit of racy dialogue, the outline of an original situation, but as literature these American plays may be regarded with pious horror. As drama they violated even the canons of their own time, the classic precepts of Lessing, who sought to draw lines of distinction between the arts. The topical themes, the breakdown into pantomime, song, the dance, acrobatics, the spectacle, all seemed to spell disintegration. Yet surely these transitory, showy effects may be read in other terms. The energy that flowed into them was not decadent but fresh. The reduction of the drama to simple elements could mean new, even primitive beginnings. If broadly drawn types appeared rather than close characterization, this need not be counted a failure. The drawing of types may represent something else altogether, an effort to study or portray or enjoy social rather than individual character. If individualism was missing in the theater, this may have been because new types were emerging, because social passions and ideas were developing as a new framework of society was being established. The stage was a meeting-place, a forum, a mirror, it was spoken journalism; it had the slightly fabulous and legendary touch and even its darker emotions had buoyancy.

Washington had argued that the stage would tend to

improve American manners, and this had become a favor-ite idea in little essays on the theater. As late as 1818, a writer in the Pittsburgh *Gazette* urged a welcome for a new company of traveling players because the stage might help to "soften" local manners. Now a rousing per-formance of the ballet called *The Highland Reel,* pro-duced with bagpipes, was not likely to inspire the suaver forms of conduct among the Scots of Pittsburgh, and it may be doubted whether the rather boisterous American stage anywhere led to a development of elegance. But the anonymous Pittsburgh writer touched upon another argu-ment of greater validity and scope, saying that the theater had "a tendency to mingle us harmoniously together." Paradoxically, the harmony was often dissident; clashes of many kinds might be contained within it; yet broad cross-sections of the population met in the theater and consistent patterns of emotion and imagination and na-tive character might be discerned there. Taste, interest and imaginative concern were in evidence outside—or within—the limits of patriotism or partisanship. In one of the most social of the arts, common modes of communi-cation and expression had quickly been established. Dur-ing these portentous years, when the structure of the new government seemed fragile, when politically the nation often seemed on the point of disruption, it might have been predicted from the theater alone that common bonds in the nation would be achieved.

IV. NEW ENGLAND

Of all the arts, the theater is supposed to have suffered most heavily from attack or suppression at the hands of the Puritans. This assumption has been repeated many times, often with a buttressing quotation from Cotton Mather, who disliked and feared the stage. It is true that, while the theater developed in other parts of the country during the colonial period, it failed to appear in New England, and Boston was the last of the larger cities to accept and establish the theater after the Revolution. Yet it may be seriously contended that the Puritans were a powerful and positive influence in the rise of the American theater. Intending nothing of the kind, they prepared a groundwork for it, and, since their influence was widely scattered by migrations from New England, this became a determining element of some breadth.

Calvinism is a highly dramatic form of faith. It rests upon a dialectic, a scheme of opposing arguments, some of which are exceedingly fine-spun. All of them are woven into the outline of a crucial situation, crucial for man. An irreducible conflict was posited, between man and God, between God and the devil, and this conflict—certainly as it was presented in the New England churches—had specific scenes or settings to which reference was constantly made: the Garden of Eden, the enticing, sensuous world, the pits of hell. The exposition of this eternal situ-

ation took highly dramatic, even theatrical forms in the
Puritan pulpit. Sermons were frequently as long as an
uncut play of Shakespeare's, and if they contained nothing like as many characters those who appeared had magnificent parts. In his sermon the minister might relate his
own struggle with the devil, with God. Members of the
congregation were sometimes denounced with explicit
stories of their conduct which were related to the great
archetypal drama of sin and salvation. Pulpit eloquence
often included passionate soliloquies, and this eloquence
was in all ways related to the eloquence of the stage. Nor
were the Puritans lacking in the theatrical sense as to
certain mundane matters, costume, for example. Though
their typical costume for both men and women was not
their invention, they heightened its expressive values by
uniformity. Those repetitious dark grays seem unobtrusive and unspectacular, even humble, in contrast to the
gay costumes of the cavaliers, but they by no means submerged the wearers. On the contrary, this costume dramatized their presence and the men crowned the effect by
tall, stiff, dark hats that made them tower over almost any
company. These costumes had practically disappeared in
the era of the Revolution, but the rich mercantile class
now dominated Boston; and, whether or not they inherited a sense of costume from the Puritan ancestry of many
of their members, they strongly possessed a sense of costume. Copley's portraits, with their magnificent portrayal
of silks, satins, ruchings, laces and proudly worn jewels,

prove it. Costume does not of course make a theater, but an instinct for expressive costume may be part of the creative impulse in the theater.

In the *New England Primer* for 1735 had appeared *A Dialogue between Christ, Youth and the Devil,* a primitive little piece that is rightly considered an early American play, perhaps the first. This was a forerunner in New England of other pioneer efforts in the American drama that came from New England. The first American play with a native theme, *Ponteach,* was written later by the famous Indian fighter of western Massachusetts and New Hampshire, Robert Rogers, commander of Rogers' Rangers. The gap in time between the *Dialogue* and *Ponteach* was a long one, some thirty years, and Rogers cannot by any imaginable standard be called a Puritan; yet within the territory dominated by Puritan thought a consistent sequence was developing. It created before the Revolution and during its course a group of plays by Mercy Otis Warren and by others who imitated her efforts, which sharply lampooned Tory leaders and formulated the main political arguments that justified the Revolution. These plays were circulated among Mrs. Warren's relatives and friends, the Otises, John Adams and his wife, John Hancock, Samuel Adams. They seem to have been more or less secretly performed in taverns, and they provoked rejoinders in the dramatic form, as in an urbane satirical piece printed in Salem, *A Cure for the Spleen.* New England was not alone in giving rise to plays of

the Revolution—they appeared in Philadelphia and elsewhere—but it is fair to say that Mrs. Warren's plays were
the most consistent and influential of them all. Simple as
they were, they had an uncompromising boldness. In
The Motley Assembly, a farce published anonymously in
1779 but almost surely by Mrs. Warren, which was widely
circulated, she made a notable advance into social satire.
Its subject was those Bostonians who feared their social
position might be damaged by association with the patriot cause. Undoubtedly these plays opened the way for
the marked sequence of political and partisan plays to
follow in later years.

Long before the law banning the theater in Massachusetts was repealed in 1793, plays were performed secretly
or under one disguise or another in Boston and in the
small towns by adventurous citizens or strolling players.
Permanent companies were soon established in Boston,
and theaters were built in rapid succession, the Federal
Street, the ambitious Haymarket, the still finer new Federal Street, designed by Bulfinch, which equaled the
Chestnut Street Theatre built by Latrobe in Philadelphia
in dignity, with the particular exquisite Bulfinch touch.
The new Federal Street Theatre was dedicated to a number of the more frivolous social pleasures: it contained
card-rooms, tea-rooms, a formal ball-room for assemblies.
John Bernard, commenting upon the Boston society that
gave substantial support to the theater, said that he could
discover little difference between this and corresponding

groups in London. "In walking along their mall"—Boston
Common—he said, "I could scarcely believe that I had
not been whisked over to St. James's Park; and in their
houses the last modes of London were observable in
every ornament or utility." Many of the people he met
had been painted by Copley. They had a rich, even a
theatrical sense of costume, not always in a low key. But
these people were by no means the only patrons of the
theater in Boston. In 1794, a theatrical company published a public "card," begging a generous people "to prevent the thoughtless or ill disposed from throwing apples,
stones, etc., into the orchestra." Surely those who engaged in these pastimes were not Puritans. Boston, like
other cities, had quickly drawn a cross-section of the public into the theater and had its gallery "boys." Neither
could the mercantile class to which Mrs. Warren belonged, those who became subjects for Copley and others,
be called Puritan in the strict sense.

Truly enough, Timothy Dwight was thundering in
these years against the seductive influence of all the arts
as he discoursed on lewdness to his students at Yale. His
address had a graphic candor, his arguments were to be
repeated by many of his young listeners in later years
as they ranged out through the country as ministers.
Lyman Beecher, for example, was among their number.
As the Puritan power waned in political government, as
formidable counter-movements in religion arose to con-
tend against it, these attacks acquired a new and explicit

violence: Puritanism was now on the defensive. But the arts against which Dwight and others inveighed continued their lively development, almost under their noses. Theatricals had flourished at Yale as in other colleges at least as early as 1784 and were to be organized there again, and from New England came a play that must be regarded as a cornerstone in the American theater.

In her plays of the Revolution, Mrs. Warren had portrayed Samuel Adams and other living individuals—some of them Tories—with energy and warmth, under thin disguises. If the characters in *The Motley Assembly* bore such unflattering names as Esquire Runt, Mrs. Flourish, Mrs. Bubble, the audience could be trusted to read their living prototypes into the play. Sketchy as these outlines of character were, they were pretty consistently drawn from life; and no doubt even their speech was mimicked when the plays were performed. Such ventures, apparently thin or transitory, sometimes create a drift or a tendency into which larger talents are swept. Royall Tyler came of much the same group to which Mrs. Warren belonged. His father had been a member of the King's Council; at Harvard, as later in the study of the law, he had been associated with those conservative Bostonians whose revolutionary principles were unmistakable and who were to become leaders of the Federalist party. John Adams was of course one of their leading figures; and young Tyler was engaged for a time to his daughter Abigail, a serious girl, who was no doubt attracted by

the charm and *esprit* of this handsome youth. They ex-
changed tokens and in 1780 entered upon a long engagement. Young Tyler was plunged into gloom when she
went to France a few years later to join John Adams, and
when after a year she returned his gifts without a word
he entered a state bordering on melancholia. Perhaps he
had been too light-hearted for John Adams.

At least his conservative principles suffered no impair-
ment. In 1787, with the rank of major, he assisted General
Lincoln in the suppression of Shays's Rebellion, traveling
into Vermont and finally to New York City on errands
related to this episode. There he saw *The School for
Scandal,* which is thought to have inspired him to try his
hand at a play. In three or four days he dashed off a
comedy, *The Contrast,* which was immediately produced
with the leading comedian Wignell in the part of Jonathan. An instant success, it was played five times in
New York and repeated in the larger cities. The second
performance was in May, when the Federal convention
opened in Philadelphia. Thus *The Contrast* was produced
against a background of momentous national events, and
it was recognized at once as a national achievement.
When it was published in 1790, Washington headed the
list of subscribers.

The theme was nationalistic, the picture social. In the
simple story, "contrast" was satirically established between the English and the American character, with triumphant virtue on the American side. On the whole, the

portraiture along these main lines was colorless: the play came to genuine life with the entrance of the minor figure of Jonathan, a Yankee. Was he a Puritan? His drawling talk may keep you guessing on that point. Though he has strayed into a theater, he ridicules the idea that he has done anything of the kind. "At the play! Why, did you think I went to the devil's drawing room? . . . Why, ain't cards and dice the devil's device, and the playhouse the shop where the devil hangs out the vanities of the world upon the tenterhooks of temptation? I believe you haven't heard how they were acting the old boy one night, and the wicked one came among them sure enough, and went right off in a storm, and carried one quarter of the playhouse with him. Oh! no, no, no! you won't catch me at a playhouse, I warrant you." He goes on graphically to describe what he saw on this excursion, but no one can be sure whether his innocence was assumed, whether he was a Puritan at heart or was satirizing the Puritan. The typical Yankee with his impassive countenance and slow ways was a prime actor. Dry, racy, imperturbable, he seemed the greenhorn, yet he could hold his own in any situation. Already known up and down the length of the land as a broad type, he had appeared in many aspects: he was a peddler well traveled in the South and even in the new West with his heavy pack. He might be a clockmaker. He whittled and tinkered, he was a roving singing-teacher; he flourished on small sailing-ships. He was pre-eminently rural, yet he was often a mechanic. It may be doubted whether, as John Adams said of others like him, he cared most for his dinner and his girl: his prime interest seemed to be exchanges of talk with the mounting crack of witty advantage or the minor personal drama of a swap—he would swap anything. The dialogue in which he so often engaged—best with another Yankee—was likely to be a prolonged swap.

The origins of his special character are lost. Sometimes he was a Puritan, more often he belonged to that independent fringe that had remained outside the strict fold, a larger contingent than is generally supposed. He flourished in strength and numbers in western Massachusetts, in Maine, New Hampshire, Vermont; on the whole, he remained outside both Calvinism and Federalism. Yet he had emerged from within the Puritan climate of belief and opinion, and his character had been ground to its subtle edges within a society governed by Puritanism. Notably he was more than himself, more than a rural New Englander; already the Yankee was the American. Yankee Jonathan—Brother Jonathan—symbolized the United States in contrast to the English John Bull; and he was to play this part for many years, when he became Uncle Sam, also a Yankee. Abroad, all Americans were being called Yankees. Jonathan in *The Contrast* was a national symbol, and he sprang into life almost full blown. Not even a prose sketch picturing the Yankee had preceded Tyler's play. Perhaps an improvisation of Yankee ways and Yankee speech had been poured into the delineations of some of the Revolutionary plays in their impromptu performances: Tyler must have seen some of them. But the most likely progenitor of his Jonathan was "Yankee Doodle." Some of Jonathan's talk has the flavor of this ballad, for which new stanzas were continually being improvised, which had already become the most widespread national song. "And did you see any folks?" queries one of the characters in the play. "Why, they come on thick as mustard," says Jonathan. His origin was not literary. Like the jigging tune of "Yankee Doodle" and its innumerable story-telling verses, he derived from the folk.

His sudden emergence full length in *The Contrast* had its oddities. In other literatures such figures had most often been established slowly, in ballads and folk-plays. When they have become tangible, writers have discovered them and they have moved into literature. No doubt this process was repeated in some measure in New England, yet even granting this to be true, granting that the traces have been lost, a marked amount of syncopation had taken place, something which in song is called the "ballad leap." The Yankee had leapt full blown into "Yankee Doodle," thence into a full-length play, and from a localism became a national folk-figure. The theater itself had followed this boldly syncopated course as it had moved from a minor to a major place in the national life, out of the sphere of private enjoyment to become suddenly—even with a rush—a public possession.

The force of such transitions appears in the career of Royall Tyler. As a well-to-do young man, he had written polite verses and dabbled in the elegant arts, and he was in a fair way to become a man of letters when he went to New York, full of melancholy. No doubt his quick turn to comedy was personal, a triumphant reaction against the humiliation of his dismissal by Abigail Adams. But where had he learned to write a play? Not from elegant models, not even from *The School for Scandal*, which seems to have given him the immediate impetus. Nor, for that matter, could he have learned from elegant models the particular dramatic art he practiced in *The Contrast*. The play was simple, naive, even primitive in its fable and its handling. But it had momentum, even now it reads and acts more than passably well because it is so direct and because of the character of Jonathan. Where had Tyler learned to know the type so well? On his errands for the suppression of Shays's Rebellion, he must have observed Yankees in some numbers but perhaps not altogether in a genial light. The escape of Shays was connived at by individuals in the rural population. Certainly Tyler did not derive from the same stratum of society as his Jonathan. There is no precise unraveling of his approaches to this portrayal; yet the character is drawn not only with accuracy but with pride and gusto. In a quiet obscure fashion the Yankee had materialized, had succeeded in impressing himself upon Tyler and others; for the play would not have been an immediate success if it had not stirred the sense of recognition in its audiences. This, the liveliest, the most positive American character in the portraiture of the stage had emerged from the life of the folk and had come from New England; still further this Yankee was already a magnified symbol of the American. Abroad all Americans were Yankees. At home "Yankee Doodle" had become a national song. A few other native folk-characters were being sketched on the stage, the backwoodsman, the Negro, the wandering Irishman who came here and never seemed to settle down, but their portraiture was slight and was long to remain so. The Yankee was the dominating figure. American characters from many backgrounds were being pictured on the stage, in increasing numbers, but they were usually pegs upon which ideas were hung: they failed to come to life. Slightly drawn as were the backwoodsman, the Negro, the Irishman, they usually captured more stirring bits of speech and song than did the merchants or lawyers or young men about town who were the formal heroes of the plays. But Jonathan exceeded them all in living qualities. In *The Contrast* he all but blotted out the other people in the play.

Tyler had by no means finished either with the stage or with the Yankee when he wrote *The Contrast*. His literary career suggests many things regarding the American imagination and the forces acting upon it in this era. For Tyler an obscure and complicated inner life had developed which no doubt in some fashion conditioned everything he wrote. What he did and failed to do was set within its framework. His pride seems to have been deeply touched by the breaking of his engagement with Abigail Adams as well as by the manner in which this was done. Surely he was not in love with little Mary Palmer whom he married. For a reason he never gave her, he insisted that their marriage should be kept secret, and when it had to be made known he absented himself from her for months at a time. When he finally gave her a home he seems to have chosen the place, the village of Guildford in Vermont, for its lack of social life. The farm near Brattleboro where the Tylers lived in later years was also secluded. They lived in the simplest fashion and they rarely had guests, yet Tyler insisted upon a rigorous formality at the table and in the house. He kept his children at a distance. Moody, fitful, he sometimes would not speak to his devoted Mary for days, then he would overwhelm her with compassionate tenderness. His journeys from home became longer and longer, his career in the law more distinguished. He became a judge and later chief justice of the Supreme Court of Vermont. He taught jurisprudence at the University of Vermont and became one of its trustees.

Immediately after the success of *The Contrast*, Tyler had dashed off another comedy, *May Day in New York*, a sprightly panoramic piece with the theme of moving day which poured upon the stage motley groups of characters. This play was produced but was not a success.

After he settled in Guildford he formed a friendship with a group at Walpole, frankly calling themselves *literati,* whose head was Joseph Dennie and whose interest was in the practice of polite letters. They wrote essays in the Addisonian style and poems in the manner of Goldsmith, and they foregathered in taverns along the Connecticut to read their effusions aloud to the group. Tyler formed a literary alliance with Dennie, and under the caption "Colon and Spondee" their essays and verse were published in *The Farmers' Weekly Museum* of Walpole, of which Dennie became the editor, a paper that had an extraordinarily wide circulation. When Dennie left for Philadelphia in 1799, to give his services to the Federalist party and later to edit his famous *Port Folio,* the tie was continued and Tyler's work appeared in this magazine.

Tyler achieved polished prose, neat verses and satire with the best of them. Yet on his long and lonely trips, during his hardly less solitary sojourns at home, he carried on writing of quite a different order, related in freshness and sometimes in theme to *The Contrast.* He wrote or adapted a number of plays, among them one that satirized a notable American trait, the passion for wild speculation. It was called *The Georgia Spec;* or *Land in the Moon,* and it had to do with land speculation at Yazoo. A journalistic piece, it could hardly have enjoyed a long life, but it was given a number of performances in Boston and New York. Tyler's other plays were equally short-lived. One was a comedy adapted from Molière, another was

based on a portion of *Don Quixote*. In spite of his strange
melancholy, his fits of seclusion, comedy seemed his forte,
yet he went off into another field altogether and wrote a
number of plays in blank verse on Biblical themes from
the Old Testament, somber and ritualistic, which remained closet drama.

All these efforts represented, in a sense, fragments of
Tyler. His main concern lay with the Yankee, with Yankee
life in its already varied forms. He never matched the
success of *The Contrast*, but he studiously and affection-
ately worked on the essential Jonathan in the midst of his
many other preoccupations. His long novel, *The Algerine
Captive*, was based on a favorite patriotic theme of the
time that was also used on the stage, that of the depre-
dations of Mediterranean pirates upon American shipping
and the capture of their crews. The insult of all this had
a sharper sting because the nation was young. The central
figure of the novel was a Yankee into whose life Tyler
imaginatively projected himself with minute detail. Cast
in the form of an autobiography, it persuasively seems an
actual record. His *Yankee in London* likewise seems a
precise account of fact and was generally taken for one
when it was anonymously published. Tyler had never
been in London but he followed his imperturbable venturesome hero with quiet fervor, in and out of taverns,
around the city, encountering Londoners over whom he
quietly triumphs by means of his wit. The humor is keen,
the style silvery-sharp: the little book is close to being

a minor classic. Nor was Tyler's concern only with the Yankee character. In a long poem, *The Chestnut Tree*, which has only recently come to light, he pictured one of the rural villages of Vermont or New Hampshire which he knew well from his travels as a jurist. When he died in 1826 he was working on an autobiographical sketch, *The Bay Boy*, which might have told us something of the well-springs of his interest and the curious tangle of his character.

Tyler belonged to a party that had no great amount of faith in the common man. He was an undeviating Federalist. If his early point of view had been shaped in Boston within the circle to which John Adams belonged, its continuity was equally clear in his later political and literary associations. In Vermont the partisan line went deep. Such men as Matthew Lyon and Anthony Haswell had suffered persecution under the Sedition Acts for their outspoken attacks upon the Federalist position: in a strict sense they were Yankees. Yet neither of them portrayed the Yankee; their literary ambitions ran in other directions. The first portrayal in American letters belonged to Tyler. Whatever his political theory, whatever the morose inner strains that seemed to separate him from a full life, he somehow kept his warm perception of common folk in New England, and he had cleaved out a primary work.

V. THE WEST

Other local characters besides the Yankee were being portrayed on the stage. A minor character called Raccoon or Cooney in the early comic opera *The Disappointment* seems to have been a frontiersman, but the piece was never performed, probably because it was too close a transcription of people and events in Philadelphia, though it was twice printed, in 1787 and in 1796, and so must have had some sort of circulation. The name of this character suggests a touch of costume that invariably belonged to the stage backwoodsman—the coonskin cap. The frontiersman might have been expected to appear first of all in the delineations of the stage, since the frontier fringed every locality; yet he did not appear until the positive inclusion of the farther West within the nation had been accomplished, and then slowly. With his braggadocio and half-Indian ways he was pictured in a few stories of the War of 1812. When a small contingent of Kentucky troops was betrayed to the Indians at the Raisin River, one of them, Seneca McCracken, who knew that defense was hopeless, was said to have got up on a stump, where he flapped his arms and crowed like a rooster. The Indians doubled up with laughter but not for long. Numbers sprang forward and the Kentuckians were wiped out. Cockolorum evidently made part of the picture even then in the midst of typical events; yet the lively typical figure with his half-Indian ways and gaudy hunting costume was not to emerge noticeably in the theater until 1822, when he appeared with a rush—to music, gusty music, a song, "The Hunters of Kentucky," which celebrated those backwoods Kentuckians, "half-horse, half-alligator," who had helped Jackson win the Battle of New Orleans.

This lively ballad was sung by an actor with a long rifle that was ominously leveled as the climactic verse was reached, "And Here Was Old Kentucky!" which was followed by a scalp-raising war-whoop. But it was some years before the frontiersman was to be pictured on the stage at greater length. Samuel Woodworth, the author of the song, was a successful playwright, as well as a prolific song-writer, but he either did not see or could not successfully draw the backwoodsman. Even this narrow presentation took place some thirty-five years after the first appearance of Jonathan in *The Contrast*.

Perhaps the Negro earned characterization on the stage because in life he was so well known as an entertainer, with songs, dances and a barbaric music of his own, on plantations, in taverns, on river-boats. He doubtless earned prominence for the obvious reason that he represented a national problem which had come to the fore when the Constitution was framed and which continued to trouble Washington, Jefferson and others. He appeared in a considerable number of full-length plays during the early years of the century, in one of which a plan to secure his freedom made an integral part of the plot. In another a Negro wench helped to bring the story to a climax. But it was not until about the time the backwoodsman emerged with a noisy song that the Negro became anything more than an anomalous shadow with a strange approximation of dialect. In 1822, on the Cincinnati stage, young Edwin Forrest, who had carefully studied the ways of an old Negro whom he had met in the town, rendered a faithful little impersonation as an entr'-acte. Perhaps less gifted actors had attempted something of the sort, and almost surely songs in blackface had been heard; but the outlined portrait still remained slight. Another quite different portrayal of the Negro appeared in Mrs. Behn's *Oronooko*, which was revived by English actors, but this was not the American Negro at all but a "noble savage," more nearly allied to the Indian who was mournfully, romantically appearing in a few American operas.

Another figure stood in the offing, the Irishman, who would inevitably have come to the fore, since he had long made a constituent part of American life and now was figuring more largely because of fresh waves of migration, but who received a special accent because of the popularity of an imported comedy, *The Poor Soldier*, which had a great vogue after the Revolution. Washington saw it a number of times with vast relish for the comic Irishman who was a leading figure. But the Irishman still remained minor on our stage. Minor too was the Pennsylvania Dutchman. The dominant figures in the long period up to 1825 were the Yankee, the backwoodsman, the Negro.

Slightly outlined though they might sometimes be, it was they who captured the liveliest bits of impersonation, speech and song. They were far more lifelike than the men and women of a higher station among whom they were thrown in plot or counterplot. There was a notable failure on the part of the playwrights in this era to give anything like a breath of life to members of the well-to-do classes, or even to portray them as distinctive groups. Individuals indeed were not a major concern of the theater at this time. Even Jonathan in *The Contrast* was not an individual whose destiny was unfolded. Tyler's treatment, though racy, was broad: Jonathan remains a firmly drawn type.

Throughout a period of some thirty-five years when the closer lineaments of character might have emerged, these portraits were persistently concerned with social rather than individual traits. They had to do with one or another racial or regional section of the new society. They came up from below. They were the folk, they belonged to the mass of the people and they belonged to the insurgent, the revolutionary class. The Yankee and the backwoodsman both had played well-recognized parts in both wars, and all three types were now in some way established in terms of conflict, contention, debate; they made the center of many a tacit argument between Puritan and anti-

Puritan, between those who moved into new country and those who clung to established societies, between races and ancestries, between the West and the East. The strongest antithesis which these stage-figures represented was an ancient one, between town and country. All of them were rural. In this they had a strong common bond, and they had another, the bond of humor. They tacitly drew themselves with humor as they talked their way through the theatrical sketches in which they appeared; and the Yankee at least used the weapon of satire.

Meanwhile, the costumes that were now a part of the American scene would have been effective on any stage. There was that of the river boatman with his hair in a queue, red shirt and stagged pants, that of the French *voyageur* who still wore the immemorial clear blue and red, the Negro with an old long-tailed coat, the Yankee with an old white hat and dusty white coat, even gray-white trousers. Other types with distinctive costumes were almost equally to the fore, the Shakers and the Quakers, both of whom moved with varying swiftness to elegance of materials. The planter of the South began to cut a figure, even though the eighteenth-century elegance which he had favored was passing. As for the Western hunter, whatever he wore was likely to be ornamented, including his gun-stock and powder-horn, which might be beautifully chased, and he sometimes donned a bright green hunting shirt that made him almost operatic. Costumes—at least masculine costumes—tended toward bril-

liance on the frontiers. The American sense of costume
was acute and was to remain so. More than costume is
required to make a theater, yet an almost ritualistic use
of costume to denote a class or an occupation has often
been a strong element in the drama—as in the Greek
drama, and persistently in the opera—outlining bold effects, achieving the suggestion of broad characters. Moreover, many of these characters could have stepped
straight on to the stage, nor would their striking appearance have been their only contribution. The hunters and
the frontiersmen could sing, most of them could dance,
and most of them could pose a story in such a fashion
that it led somewhere, into some further dialogue or
knockdown action. These men of the back country
seemed born actors; they had a sense of display, the theatrical temperament. They could instantly eradicate expression from their faces; the blank countenance, the poker
face, the dead pan were already American accomplishments, and by no means confined to the hardy frontiersmen. The Yankee of the rural districts could match and
outmatch any of them in quiet acting, and his daily wear
had its low-keyed theatrical aspects, with its whitey
blues and grays and occasional worn butternut browns.
Adopted first for practical reasons—indigo and butternut
and linsey-woolsey were at hand—he seems to have retained them because he liked to keep things as they were;
and, as he emerged as a well-known type and realized his
audience—in taverns, on local roads, on his travels into

the West—he seems to have kept his costume with pride. Like the hunters and the river boatmen, he apparently enjoyed—as any actor would—creating a sensation by his looks, his lingo, his repartee and even his songs; for the Yankee too was full of ballads.

If the people of the theater made a bright ribbon of color and character through the country, they were nicely matched by many of their audience. Audience and players were counterparts in a broad fashion, mingling together at many points, both effervescent, changeable in moods, tending toward overflow. Something incalculable belonged to this stream of life outside the theater and in it. It enclosed lawless forces of the imagination, as in the Gothic plays, anomalies as in those in which the Indians figured, and a great cascade of conflicting political and even philosophical ideas.

Thus the passion for the classic that arose in the theater and elsewhere was also an anomaly: it may even be considered a phase of a romantic passion for the exploratory, the remote, the unaccustomed, the new. Nothing could have seemed more distant from a frontier country than the civilizations of Greece and Rome; but their literature had been part of our higher education from the founding of the first universities in the colonial period. Greece and Rome were rediscovered as the ancestral republics, closer by far to the American people than the countries of their origin. Jefferson, Hamilton and Madison had discussed the faults and failures of Sparta, Rome and Carthage, but their arguments enhanced the parallels. Classic architecture had come with a rush. Classic oratory was widely studied: such small instructive works as the *Columbian Orator* provided practice-pieces for the young that abounded in classic allusions. Strangely scattered among poetic Indian place-names on many a frontier were others of classic origin: Athens, Rome, Carthage, Ionia, Ypsilanti. Classic themes reached the stage slowly, but they came at least in 1819 with the first performance in this country, after a considerable triumph in London, of John Howard Payne's *Brutus,* a synthetic but fairly powerful work whose popularity here was augmented by the writer's early fame as the infant Roscius and his long friendship with Washington Irving. His career had begun precociously in New York, and he was considered an American genius, an idea that was later to be reinforced by his writing of "Home, Sweet Home." The classic ideal was the republican ideal; and no doubt something akin to a wish for the classic balance and calm—in the midst of all the turmoil and uncertainty of pioneering—belonged to the American embodiments of this ideal.

Meanwhile, traveling theatrical companies had moved into the West very soon after the Revolution, on the heels of the early settlers. They followed pretty much the route afterward taken by the Erie Canal, and later they traveled by the Canal. Then in skiffs they would float down the Genesee, or, preferably, the Allegheny, through always unbroken forests. Often they sent one skiff ahead to spy

out the land. If the people in the clearing seemed hos-
pitable, a bit of white cloth would be tied to the branch
of an overhanging tree for a signal to the actors who
followed. If the people seemed rough, the scouting party
would hang out a red flag. If they were fortunate, the
company would stop at a tiny cluster of huts or cabins
and play in a loft or barn. There was usually no curtain.
The place would be tiny, perhaps twelve by sixteen, with
a few plain benches for the boxes and pit, and potatoes
hollowed out for candlesticks. There were no dressing-
rooms, and often an actor would have to wear one costume throughout, and, as there was always a great
amount of doubling in these productions, there must have
been some confusion—or else some superlative acting—if
one character was to be distinguished from another.
Sometimes not even tallow dips were to be found to stick
in the potato candlesticks, and candles were improvised
out of some fat and old linen. One company rattled
through *Richard III* in the dark. The effect must have
been a little eerie, with the rustling of a deep forest outside, the river flowing by and the dark huddle of the
audience.

The costumes were by no means opulent. They were
carried in baskets, and, if one looks at theatrical photo-
graphs even of a time as late as the eighties, one observes
that the dresses of the actresses were often badly creased,
for everything went into those baskets, not only costumes
and hats and jewelry, but all the personal treasures of the

actors, and with these early companies sometimes one basket had to do for the whole troupe. At Greensburg in the early eighteen-twenties, a company put on *Richard III*. Richard wore a common soldier's coat. The royal Henry pranced out in a Scotch kilt. Richmond wore a short sailor-jacket and Turkish pantaloons, with a large damask tablecloth thrown over his shoulders. There were only three in this company, and, since there was no curtain, there was a good deal of difficulty in getting the dead off the stage so that the play could go on.

On these journeys the actors often started with next to nothing, and the towns along the way were very small. They had to take the luck of adventurers and were chronically in difficulties when they reached the great gateway into the West, Pittsburgh. Often stranded there, they would hire themselves out for small jobs, such as sign-painting or portrait-painting—almost any actor could bend his talents to do a little painting. They often ran into debt for board and lodgings. They had to borrow money. Sometimes they tried to slip out of town without paying their debts. Naturally, the constables were swift and wary in a great meeting-place like Pittsburgh, where there were many floating characters whose antecedents and intentions were unknown. But the actors too were wary, and they had one advantage over the constables. They were used to making quick changes. They could assume new characters. They could face a constable in the street and he would not know them. Once, when the con-

stables were waiting outside a theater to seize an actor
after a performance of *Hamlet,* he popped into the grave
at the end and was never seen again, at least in Pittsburgh. Once an actor put on a benefit performance for
himself in Pittsburgh, hoping to raise enough to clear his
debts. The performance was a bumper; the house was
jammed. But the creditors had all applied for tickets,
thinking that was all they were likely to get. Only about
thirty dollars was taken in at the box-office, and the actor
was obliged to hire himself out as a wax figure and stand
for hours immovable in a window in order to work out
his debt.

From Pittsburgh, these traveling companies went down
the Ohio in flatboats, floating in great arks along the most
romantic and beautiful highway of pioneer days. They
took a hand at the oars, cooked their own food and often
hoisted their scenery for sails. As this scenery was always
painted on both sides, the sails might show at once the
battlements of a great castle and a street in Rome, or perhaps a bit of forest to match the forests along the banks
of the river. Occasionally the actors would rehearse in
costume as they floated along, to the wonderment of
others on the river. One pictures them crossing swords
or speaking the poetry of Shakespeare in that lovely
idyllic setting.

They landed at little towns. Lexington and Louisville
had theaters founded early in the century and welcomed
the best actors. Often the actors left their flatboats and

pushed far into the back country of Kentucky and down into Tennessee, traveling over the Cumberlands, reaching remote settlements that had never seen a play or an actor. They even wandered into that wild territory bordering the Mississippi where the famous Murrell gang held sway, horse-thieves, murderers and stealers of slaves. However, as the purses of the actors were usually light, they seldom attracted robbers. But they had other troubles. They often ran into the counter-attraction of revivals and were obliged to wait until a great camp-meeting had ended and a reaction had set in, before people would come out to see a play. The charms of faro and other gambling-games were rivals of the theater, often luring every male in the place, and of course women did not go to the theater alone in those days. They ran into the cholera and were sometimes fatally stricken. Still they pushed on, making their way south into the wilds of Alabama and Mississippi. Sometimes they crossed the strip of territory belonging to the Creeks, and, since the Creek War was still fresh in memory, this was a fairly lively experience. One company was seized by a band of warriors and forced to play to them. In a town further south a band of Creeks were visiting when some actors came to town, and, since the company was very small, and the play they wished to put on demanded numbers, they rashly decided to employ the Indians as supers. It was the highly popular old play, *Pizarro*. The Indians became more and more excited as the play went on, and finally got entirely out of hand and broke into an active war-dance on the stage. The actors and the audience fled in terror.

In one little town in the South a troupe played in a graveyard. Sometimes theaters were built overnight to receive them. They traveled by steamboat up the small rivers to find audiences, for steamboats threaded their way up the smaller rivers even in these early days, fragile little boats that could practically climb a tree or leap over a log. They could scarcely have been called safe. The firepot was an open affair in the middle of the boat, and the very simple steamworks often blew up. They carried cotton for the most part, which was highly inflammable, and a few curious travelers along with the actors. There was little of early American life these actors did not see. They made their way to Natchez, with its beautiful old houses, Portobello, Montrose and others. Strolling companies often played in the ballrooms of these houses, often before an audience which included the house Negroes as well as the whites. Then there was the wicked Natchez under the Hill, with its throngs of desperadoes and gamblers, where the actors often also played. And there was the trip down the river to New Orleans, a Mecca for actors rarely reached by ordinary strollers. For there the best Parisian actors appeared, and there was no place for casual players. Small companies usually turned north again at Natchez, by steamboat, when they could afford it, but more often following the famous Natchez Trace on horseback or on foot, up into Tennessee. Then they might strike the Cumberland and float down that beautiful river to the Ohio. The Ohio, and then the Mississippi, remained the great theatrical highway.

One thinks of the showboat as belonging to the sixties and seventies, because of Edna Ferber's story, but it came into existence long before that, in the late twenties and early thirties. It was invented by the famous Chapman family and started on the Ohio, though the Chapmans also played along the Mississippi. They even went up the wild Arkansas, and the still wilder White River, pulling themselves upstream by the process known as bush-whacking—that is, literally climbing up the river by clutching bushes and then walking to the stern of the boat. Sometimes they were towed by a steamer.

Their showboat was an ark, or a flatboat, rigged up as a theater and a home. It was very neat and comfortable, and the Chapmans were often more intent on fishing than on playing. Sometimes they would stop a play because catfish were biting, and the villain, who was expected to come on and die, had cast his line over while offstage. There were so many Chapmans that they made a company all by themselves, and they were gifted actors, enormously absorbed in the gaieties and adventures of their precarious existence and absorbed in their own extraordinary family life. They seemed to care very little for fame and have left no record of themselves behind, but the family lineage goes back to the first production of *The Beggar's Opera* in London, in which one of their ancestors took a leading part. A patriarchal elder Chapman presided over the large family in America on their show- boat, and they were all talented. But the two who stand out are William and Caroline. From many sources we know that they both had the indefinable essence of style in their acting, sheer style, for neither of them had looks. Caroline had no beauty, quite the contrary; she was tall, gawky, almost homely. But they were steeped in the theater. They sang and they danced and, when necessary, they could apply the irresistible touch of burlesque. There were so many of the Chapmans that they could cast al- most any play without assistance, and they were also very clannish. They had a secret language which they used among themselves when they appeared among other ac- tors in the greenroom, when they descended upon New York, as they sometimes did, or later in California. With delicacy and spirit at their command, they could also deal out grape and canister to rowdies who attacked their boat far up the Arkansas. They were even highly literary, and the older William Chapman was really learned. Yet life on the showboat precisely suited them, and it may be doubted whether even the restless Caroline—a wit if there ever was one—was ever happier than in those floating years on the Western rivers.

The Jeffersons were another such family, belonging to this period. Those who saw Joe Jefferson as Rip Van Winkle are not likely to forget him; his memory seems to be perennially green. But this Jefferson belonged mainly to the eighties and nineties. We hear less of the boy, the struggling young actor who went traveling through all this country with his gifted parents. Cornelia Jefferson was a very beautiful woman and an accomplished actress. Her husband had a fine presence and a notable emotional power. Cornelia Jefferson's son by a former marriage, Charles Burke, who died young, was apparently something of a genius. With a small company, the Jeffersons traveled all through this new West along the familiar routes. They had the familiar trials. They crossed the Mississippi from Illinois on the ice in a sleigh when the ice was melting and bent and heaved before their eyes. Once the older Jefferson was obliged to take an engagement in an Alabama town, and the family had to separate. They were to meet further along, and Mrs. Jefferson with her family set out in a wagon with the children. She had no money, though she expected some at the end of the journey, but the driver became suspicious and put the whole family out on the road in a lonely place. The lovely Cornelia Jefferson had to make her way for miles on foot as best she could through wild country.

Then there were the Drakes, a famous theatrical family, who founded the first theater in Kentucky. And there were the Booths, but of them there is much more to say.

VI. THE ELDER BOOTH

No man can quite sum up an age or a type, yet Junius Brutus Booth embodied many of the strolling figures in this free period, with much of the conflicting emotion and humor that were given so loose a rein. He enlarged the stamp and kept something of his own. Like any great actor, Booth comprised many characters, but he made an invariable choice of those possessing scale. More than any other figure in the American theater, he expressed its major phases; yet his life, so closely folded into the life of its time, may be read for its strange undercurrents alone. The curious circumstance was that pursuing his own dark destiny he could so indicate main streams. He was an acutely edged individual: he was also an archetype. No one was quite like him, yet he comprised the sum of many men.

When he came to this country in 1821, he was only twenty-five, but honors of the stage were thick upon him because of his stormy rivalry with Edmund Kean. This had been as swift and intensive as a duel, and Booth, much the younger, had emerged transcendent. He had established himself as a tragedian of the first rank. The complexities of his personal life had already begun. He had become an actor against the opposition of his father, and during a visit to the continent he contracted, at the age of eighteen, a secret marriage in Brussels: two children were born of this marriage. But on his return to London he had fallen in love with a flower-girl of the Covent Garden Market, his Mary Ann, whose delicate exotic beauty, simplicity, devotion and serenity make her seem a figment out of a romantic novel. She actually seems to have possessed these qualities, and she needed them; in particular, she needed serenity as an artist needs genius. No question as to Booth's loyalty seems to have arisen; he adored her. His marriage was kept secret even after his wife's arrival in London, and it is a question whether Mary Ann knew of this marriage until years later. For a time Booth maintained two households. Then he carried Mary Ann away on an idyllic trip to the Azores and extended this on an impulse to the United States.

Landing unheralded in Norfolk, Booth cast about for a few engagements and had no trouble finding them. His fame had spread, but he was still hardly more than a boy, and, when he rushed in late for a rehearsal at Petersburg wearing a dusty straw hat and a short jacket, having walked the twenty-five miles from Richmond, he had difficulty convincing the company that he was really the great Booth.

Apparently Booth was always indifferent to his reputation; even then he was pursuing a secret path of his own. He tried to obtain the post of keeper of the light at Cape Hatteras, perhaps for its stark symbolism, perhaps because its isolation would have afforded him a hiding-place. When managers intervened, he leased a tract of

wild forest in Maryland, "for a thousand years," as the
deed said. Booth would have liked such an extension into
eternity. This was "The Farm," which became an eighteenth-century French philosopher's dream of a farm:
Crèvecœur or Chateaubriand might have contrived it. On
all sides lay an even deeper forest, with footpaths of the
Algonquins and mysterious rings where grass never grew,
and beyond was a great swamp with bright lilies. Everywhere was the sound of falling water. Here Booth built
a log cabin, plastered white inside and out with bright
red window-sashes and doors, which looked like a house
in an opera against the great back-drop of forest. The
hand of Rousseau was the shaping hand in this whole
scene, and here all nature was sacred, even the trees. Only
fallen timber and brushwood were used for fires, and the
partridge, the wild boar and the blacksnake could roam
at will. Flesh for food was forbidden in this household.
Even in his brief London years Booth had anticipated
this preoccupation with the philosophy of nature by playing the lead in one of the American plays picturing a
phase of Indian history. He continued to take these parts,
with their philosophical undertones, and was known to
introduce the popular "Song of Alknoomok"—or the Cherokee lament, as it was sometimes called—somewhat irrelevantly into his plays and entr'actes. He revived
Oroonoko, playing the savage African chief in bare feet,
a departure that was considered wildly original. Booth
played the part with disdainful fire, disdainful of a

vaunted civilization. Though Oroonoko was black, the theme was that of the Indian plays, celebrating nature and natural instinct.

At "The Farm," these ideas mingled with the classic ideal, which also had a tangible embodiment in the person of Booth's father, old Richard Booth, who followed his son to America, apparently reconciled to Booth's position on the stage. Tall, slender, habitually wearing a plain black coat, knee breeches, silver shoe-buckles and a queue, Richard Booth had long been deeply rooted in republican ideas. As a young man, he had attempted to leave England to fight in the American revolution. In this he had been unsuccessful, but he had insisted that visitors in his London house uncover before the picture of Washington; and he was deep in the analogies between the United States and the classic civilizations. The name of his son Junius Brutus was a symbol of his convictions and preoccupations; and in the forest retreat, amid the tangle of wild land, to the sound of falling water, he wrote odes to liberty—declamatory odes inevitably, worked on biographies of classic heroes, began a translation of the *Aeneid* with a view to its adaptation to the stage, and was fond of repeating the lines that begin *Dulce et decorum est pro patria mori*. A certain inconsistency appeared in this projection of classic republicanism and the philosophy of nature. Old Richard Booth used to march to the village attended by a gigantic black. But the Booths owned no slaves, they only borrowed or rented them; and in terms of ideas at least they were consistent. They read Pythagoras, reinforcing their belief that no flesh should be eaten; they read Locke and Shelley, particularly *Queen Mab*. They must have extended their reading into some of the great myths that celebrated nature, for one of Booth's children was named for the Norse goddess of fertility Frigga. With a sufficient sense of natural scale, she was also named for a continent—Asia Frigga. The republican strain was continued in the family when Booth named his youngest son after John Wilkes, who was a remote connection. This was the ill-starred John Wilkes Booth, who was also an actor, like his older brother Edwin. Nine children were born to Junius Brutus Booth and Mary Ann.

Away from "The Farm," and outside the theater, Booth sustained his republican principles in the eccentric fashion for which he became noted. In conspicuously simple garb, he would take a calf and his surplus vegetables to Baltimore and sit for hours at the market. He consorted with sailors in water-front taverns, looking like a middy ashore in a glazed cap and roundabout. He could "drink with a tinker in his own language," and often did so. He habitually consorted with humble folk, and it is only a question whether this was a matter of republican theory or expressed a submerged desire to humble himself. Once, when he had begun to drink more and more heavily, he pawned himself for the price of a drink and then stood in the pawnshop-window, bearing the tag with its small

price upon it, not only humble but humiliated. Undoubtedly, many of these ventures embodied obscure emotions
by which Booth was tormented. His letters to his father,
when he was away from "The Farm" on theatrical tours,
were filled with a confused self-reproach as well as with
the gentlest tenderness. No doubt, the strain of his early
conflict with Kean, when Booth was hardly more than a
boy, had tended to warp him out of his natural orbit; and
the conflict was continued when Kean came to the United
States. Besides, in spite of his libertarian principles, the
position of Mary Ann must have weighed upon him. More
than once he returned to England, taking Mary Ann and
their children with him, playing to packed houses, continuing the bitter rivalry with Kean, avoiding what might
have seemed inevitable complications inasmuch as his
wife was living in London.

It was inevitable that Junius Brutus Booth should have
gone forth from his idyllic retreat. Neither his classicism
nor his tranquillity was perfectly established; and the
overflow of his immense histrionic power was bound to
carry him out of solitude. He was steeped in his parts as
few actors were, as if they were portions of himself, inevitably appearing at the surface; his concentration and
control were prodigious. Spare, muscular, with a broad
neck, an ample chest, Booth looked the classical, the
Roman republican part; he moved on the stage with a
quietly imperial air. His hair was dark, his eyes a deep
blue, his pallor so fine and clear that he looked in mo-

ments of repose as though carved from alabaster. His
figure had a defect, bandy legs, but he was able to disguise the awkward outline by the dignity of his stance
and the grace of his movements. He seemed the very
embodiment of a serene and powerful balance, of the
classic ideal. Yet he could plunge from such a play as
Payne's *Brutus* headlong into the dark romantic dramas
that Americans had adopted as their own, *The Iron Chest,
Pizarro, Venice Preserved.* Their fearful emotions, their
desperate tensions, their themes of terror, revenge and
hideous ambition seemed his own. His fellow-actor Jefferson said that as Sir Giles Overreach, in the last scene,
Booth's face as he realized that he could not reach Marrall
had the look of an uncaged tiger. One actor of his company declared that his eyes emitted strange and supernatural lights. His cheeks quivered; his thin lips were
drawn back in animal rage over his teeth. In other parts
he flushed visibly with anger or shame. In the midst of a
death-scene his face was known to turn ghastly white.
Certain critics thought that he thus commanded his own
pulses, others that his participation was so complete as to
induce the physical effects of the emotions portrayed. The
familiar tale of Booth's fighting Richmond off the stage,
out the door and up an alley might seem to lend color to
the theory of an uncontrolled submersion; yet in this episode Booth may have been quite aware of what he was
doing. He may have been propounding with fury one of
his practical jokes, perhaps because of the pretenses of

the actor who played the other part. Certainly proof abounds that in his prime and indeed even in his more distraught moments Booth possessed a detachment that joined perfectly with his emotional powers. Jefferson told of seeing him back-stage, where Booth began a story; he was called to his part, played the tragic episode with unusual fire, and the moment he stepped from the stage dropped back into the story at precisely the point he had left it. Delicate passages were at his command as well as terrific ones. As Octavian in *The Mountaineers* he tenderly portrayed the emotions of discovery; and in that part made a fine diversion from the usual embrace, locking the fingers of his uplifted hand within the fingers of Floranthe. And he was one of the few actors who declined to mar the impression which they have created by curtain-calls. The temptation must have been great, for few actors in the country at the time enjoyed anything approaching Booth's popularity. But he maintained his purpose, in spite of the prayers and imprecations of managers and the thunder of applause. Once indeed he made an exception, after playing Octavian, and consented to come forward as the curtain was finally descending on an empty stage. But, with unmistakable clarity, he still maintained the melancholy beauty of the character, so that his appearance seemed a last echo of the part.

Or was it humility that kept him from enjoying the familiar tributes? Booth's character was strangely mixed. There was arrogance in it, compounded with abasement.

Traveling, he chose rooms in the humblest quarter of the town, in tenements on narrow streets or shabby lanes, sometimes up several flights of stairs, with the plainest possible accommodations. His daughter's earliest recollection of her father was of seeing him on his knees before a rough sailor who had asked alms at the door. The man had a badly wounded leg; Booth brought him into the house, and washed and bandaged the wound with tender care. His standing in a pawnshop-window after he had pawned himself for the price of the drink was no unconscious accident; the strange episodes in which Booth took part nearly always had a definite design. When Charles Kean came to Baltimore in 1831, Booth, who was then at the very climax of his early career in this country, offered to play the second actor with Kean as Hamlet. No part could be less telling, though Booth gave the lines great beauty of delivery. Apparently he wished to give the son of his early rival the greatest possible advantage, but was this alone his purpose? His choice of the part of the second actor seemed to suggest a deliberate other meaning. What Booth's conclusions were about Edmund Kean was never known—his comments were always deeply respectful—but he seemed either ironical or assertively truthful in assuming the part of an inferior actor in a mock theatrical troupe. On another occasion, after a marked success in one of his tragic roles, he stood in the wings and listened to an admirable singer, who gave a number before the after-piece. Booth, who could neither sing nor dance, sought him later in the refreshment-room, stretched himself on the floor, placed one of the singer's feet upon his own neck, held it there for a few moments, and then silently departed.

Whether his humility sprang from a deliberate equalitarian faith, which challenged any pride of place, or whether it had its origins in early and obscure personal relations, no one can tell: the records, as often among actors, are too scant. Certainly his youthful emotional life had been checkered. Before he was twenty he had had confused experiences. Once he saw three men guillotined, and his youthful marriage had ended badly. There had been besides the impact of his phenomenal youthful success and the public conflict with Kean. All this was stimulus enough for strange emotions and a wild self-deprecation offered to a highly charged nature. The extraordinary circumstance was that out of this brief and confused tutelage he had emerged with so fine a concentration and control. Nor can it be said that his experiences in America further shattered him: rather he found here an ample scope both for the highly emotionalized character of his genius and for the theatricals on a wider scale which he soon chose to play. His most sympathetic observers believed that his early eccentricities were assumed. Hamlet was his favorite part. Like Hamlet he was thought to have put an antic disposition on to conceal "supernatural emotions" or in reaction against them. It was not until later years that his eccentricities took on the tinge of madness.

Dark gusty plays like *Pizarro* seemed peculiarly Booth's own. He even wrote one, *Ugolino,* in which the direst human emotions were compounded. Its writing was crude, it had no success, but in another manner Booth found a means of expressing a similar strain of feeling. He built a Gothic manor at Bel Air in Maryland with gabled, mullioned windows, recesses and dark passages. Deserting "The Farm," he brought his family there. It was a small castle of Udolpho, a house in which Poe would have liked to wander; and indeed young Poe was no great distance away, absorbing, as had Booth, the moods and preoccupations of the so-called Gothic in the arts, which had traveled across the sea by way of novels and plays, with its paganism, its medievalism, its stresses upon the eerie. Haunted houses, haunted men, these were Gothic themes, and Booth embodied them both. He by no means abandoned the cult of the natural, but he embraced the cult of the supernatural. He ventured into Rosicrucianism and studied the occult in many aspects. Undoubtedly, his exaltation of nature belonged to the deism that spread in this country through the works of the eighteenth-century philosophers of France, which became part of a movement against organized religion; and this kind of supernaturalism was seized upon by some of the new, wayward religious groups that had broken away from the established churches. The Gothic movement in the arts was European in its origins, but many a movement had come here without results, and

Gothicism took root here because many medieval elements still lingered in American beliefs, superstitions and customs. Supernaturalism had been a potent force since the days of witchcraft in New England. A belief in supernatural powers and presences had governed the long chain of revivals up and down the country. These powers were exalted by many a new small sect developing in the back-country and in the West.

Booth was religious in his way. He could deliver the Lord's Prayer in such a fashion as to move his listeners to tears and perhaps to make them shudder, but his convictions were set against formal religion and its exponents. His mournful burial of wild pigeons on one of his Western journeys was partly an expression of natural philosophy, partly a bit of macabre humor and partly a prank on a minister. The slaughter of these birds had been ruthless and great flocks were brought to earth within a few hours. Booth called a minister to his room in a small Western tavern, saying that he wished to discuss the burial of a friend. While the minister respectfully listened, Booth talked of the purity and worth of this dead friend, then, turning, drew back a sheet on his bed and disclosed a heap of slaughtered pigeons and eerily declaimed *The Ancient Mariner*. The minister, who recognized the meaning of this ceremony, departed feeling like the wedding guest. Booth then bought a lot in the cemetery and buried the pigeons with a public service, at which he declaimed poetry whose theme was nature.

On one occasion, traveling on foot to a small Kentucky hamlet, where he had an engagement, Booth met an officer on horseback with a runaway slave. He then rode away on a horse at the door of the inn where they all paused, declaring when he was overtaken that he was a notorious horse-thief named Lovett. In the Louisville jail he was turned over to a stupid turnkey who examined all his clothes with care to make sure of his identity and counted the prisoners before locking him up. When the jailer left for the market, Booth escaped and confronted him there. "I never saw you before," said Booth in sepulchral tones. The turnkey ran back to the jail to count his prisoners, but Booth was there before him. Returning to the market, he encountered Booth again, and again found Booth in his cell when he reached the jail. Tiring of this joke, Booth tried another; he first feigned illness and then death, and was carried from the jail in a coffin, emerging to play his deferred engagements in Louisville and in neighboring hamlets. But his interest in Lovett, the horse-thief, was by no means over. When at length Lovett was captured, Booth traveled far to see him and contrived to be locked in a cell with him the night before he was hanged. Lovett bequeathed him his skull, which Booth accepted and even cherished. He used this in playing *Hamlet*.

Booth must have carried mental burdens that he was unable to throw off. His eccentricities increased, he drank more and more heavily, he was called mad, he flaunted engagements. He indulged in drolleries on the stage that had no place in the play and only maintained his position because his acting was really great. But his madness like his genius assumed consistent patterns. He had stolen the horse to play a prank on an officer who was taking the Negro back to slavery because he liked pranks but at bottom because slavery violated the philosophy of nature in which he believed. His concern with Lovett was part of the same philosophy, which contended that civilization was evil. The thief—of the lowest order—exemplified its effects: the fault was not with him but with society. Booth had a genuine liking for the macabre, and something grotesque or cruel often ran through his elaborate pranks; those which he practiced on his fellow-actors were likely to be brutal, but few were lacking in ideas or wit. He usually lampooned meanness or timidity, and in this too he was consistent, for such qualities diminished the stature of man, who in his natural state was inherently noble.

He moved more and more into the West, often as in a trance, often playing best to thin houses, as willing to play in a frontier village as in the larger cities. In New Orleans he played *Talma* to riotous applause, but it was Tennessee that he loved best. Its small towns were set in the midst of a country with a wild tang. There he knew the unlettered Davy Crockett, famed as the great hunter of the West, who was already on the way to become a backwoods statesman. Booth could hardly have missed the fact that Crockett exemplified the natural man. There he became friends with Sam Houston, who had his own strange inner entanglements and who possessed many of the tastes and ideas and imaginative strains of Booth himself. With Houston a philosophy of nature was not an abstraction; he too had practiced it, early finding a place within the great Cherokee nation; he knew the language, the tribe were already his own people; this alliance was to govern his whole life. In Houston was focused that dual strain of ideas that had appeared on the stage and in the life of the nation, exalting the Indian—the natural man—and equally the civilization of Greece and Rome. The two concepts were poles apart; yet Booth had entertained them both and an early glimpse of Houston shows him on a river island among the Cherokees, reading Pope's translation of the *Iliad*.

The two fast friends traveled up and down the country together, wearing Indian warpaint and feathers, and enjoyed the perennial American masquerade. At wayside taverns—in this costume—they would match each other in another field of display, that of eloquence, reciting declamatory speeches or poetry through whole evenings to any audience that would listen. On one occasion Booth recited speech after speech on the theme of liberty from plays, and Houston repeated them after him. Booth managed to visit Washington whenever Houston was there as a member of Congress, and on one occasion, when Houston had spoken from the floor, rushed down from

the gallery to join him, exclaiming with ardor, "Take my
laurels!" Nor was the gesture an empty one: in the middle
eighteen-twenties, theatrical managers in Washington
were complaining that plays failed in the national capital
because gifts belonging to the stage were so freely employed by the nation's representatives and senators. Yet
Booth could command an audience in the theater there
as elsewhere, in spite of eccentricities, in part because of
them. In the runaway dash and splendor of the theater of
this era, in its consistent preoccupation with ideas, he
sustained a continuous part, even entering upon its ruder
humor in the after-pieces. Only in one respect did he
swerve from its color and character: he was not musical.
Booth could not sing. But his other powers were almost
unexampled in this time, and before him still stretched
years in which, still tormented, often only a magnificent
ruin, he was to follow the frontier as it moved farther
and farther westward, playing the antique Roman, weaving together his faith in nature, his sense of the supernatural and of evil and his abstract belief in liberty.

A portrait of Booth in the late forties gives a clue to an
attitude which seemed to underlie his last phase.
Throughout his career he had sallied forth again and
again on his personal enterprises, showing in public the
patterns of his strange ideas and convictions, and he
seemed now to be telling the multitude that knew him
through and through the meaning of these evil parts that
he assumed. He seemed to be saying that *he* was evil, that

he comprised all the wretched and desperate, tragic traits which they embodied. The face that looks out from the old daguerreotype is shameless, battered and indifferent, yet in the tired eyes there is a look of irony which no tragedy could remove. The whole posture speaks, as Booth leans carelessly back and gazes out upon the world.

Richard Booth died at the end of a long lifetime. Two of Booth's most beloved children had died. Peacock, his piebald horse, had gone. The place that Booth's gentle wife played in his existence can perhaps never be known; she emerges only as a delicate shadow, the mother of his nine children. He still returned to his family, as if bound by a tether, but the tether grew longer and longer, and in his later years he was accompanied by his son Edwin. It was inevitable that he should finally have gone to California. It was not only that his oldest son, Junius Brutus, had gone before and was engaged in theatrical enterprises on the Coast, where the theater from the first had so richly flourished. The attraction of the rolling Western movement, which the elder Booth had always felt, was bound in any case to have drawn him to this new highly colored manifestation. He embarked on the *Brother Jonathan,* in the early autumn of 1852.

On the morning of departure, Booth stood watching the transportation of boxes and barrels from the pier to the ship. He was annoyed by the slow movements of a surly seaman. Booth urged him to work more quickly;

the man worked more slowly. "What are you employed for?" asked Booth. "Who are you?" "I am a thief," replied the seaman in a vicious tone. "Give me your hand, comrade, I am a pirate!" exclaimed Booth. It was not, however, with the old broad touch that he embarked upon his engagements in California. He seemed somber and indifferent, yet, as he played, the familiar fire broke forth. With his deep and bitter tragedies he drew to himself the gay and riotous little city of San Francisco. He had given in Boston not long before his departure some of the finest of his Shakespearean performances; his great powers always had their great resurgences. Now once again his high tragic revelations grew: his audiences, which had been trained by a succession of fine actors, were entranced: they might have guessed that they were watching the all but final manifestations of a strange career. In Sacramento, Booth's appeal was less deep; perhaps his gift faltered; it seemed rather that the rougher audiences there were unready for tragedy because it lay at closer hand, in the wild experiences of the mines. Again Booth played in San Francisco to an impassioned enthusiasm, and then departed. His general air off the stage seemed to be that of a dogged submission to routine, but he made a significant gesture, as if to say that he was abdicating—he gave his jeweled diadem to his son Junius. Edwin was to remain in California. The circumstance was strange, since his father thought little of his son's histrionic powers; it was strange too since the boy had been his almost necessary companion. The shock of his father's death a few weeks later was deep for Edwin; it may have spelled remorse, it must have meant the plumbing of a deep personal relation. It was only a few years later that Edwin Booth emerged as a tragic actor; and the part in which he was to excel was his father's great part of Hamlet, that complex record of a deep and uncertain filial tie. As his father had enacted the tragic bond, so did he: the difference was that the Hamlet of Edwin Booth lacked humor.

Across the continent was another son who, by tragedy of a deeper kind, was to link Junius Brutus Booth with the future. The episode some dozen years later at Ford's Theater seemed a thin, high-pitched echo of those symbolic bits of personal drama which the elder Booth had been wont to contrive. In John Wilkes Booth this act of folly was only a shallow assertion, but the reverberant tragedy was something of which his father could hardly have dreamed, even with his encompassment of tragedy. There had been a fiber of connection between Lincoln and the elder Booth in 1852 and earlier. It was in the regions which Lincoln knew best that Booth had exerted his great spell; here he had emerged into a legendary figure. He had deepened that great pool of emotion from which Lincoln drew, had heightened a sense of the grotesque there which was not far from Lincoln's humor and which was part of his own.

It was to the West once more that Junius Brutus Booth

turned at last, landing in New Orleans, where he played with that brilliance which had often been an accompaniment of his inner turmoil, and then taking passage for Cincinnati on a Mississippi river boat. He was cold, he drank the river water and was taken ill. He let no one know; there was no physician on board and he died. The delicate, shadowy Mary Ann Booth, his wife, came to Cincinnati for the body. Booth was buried at Baltimore. His face under the glass window was so lifelike that it was thought he had fallen into a trance. His eyes, now gray, were partly visible; his lips, which had color, were smilingly closed. He wore a look of tranquillity. A great procession followed him to the grave, of all sorts and conditions, blacks and whites, men he had known along the waterfront and others who could measure the subtler shades of his poetic expression.

Early American Music

HARDLY waiting for the guns of the Revolution to grow silent, foreign travelers hastened across the sea to view the new nation in its first infancy, as a spectacle, as a dubious adventure, as the hope of the world; and they heard the strains of music everywhere. Some of them thought that the returning fife and drum corps had stirred an admiring populace by their martial tunes, and that thus enlivened the American people had kept on singing and playing.

No doubt the fife, in particular, suited the mood of the moment. A lively instrument, it could be gay, triumphant; fife-music could also be comical, it started feet moving, it awakened voices. It was heard in the midst of the many celebrations of peace. Its shrill notes took the pattern of the many marches devised for Washington's entry into New York or Boston or other cities. Some of these were popular for at least two generations; at theaters other music by the orchestra might be interrupted by catcalls from the gallery demanding a Washington march long after Washington's death. Songs of praise celebrating his deeds and his character were written, songs for his birthday and "liberty songs." With them all might be heard the high clear notes of the fife. For many years small books of fife tunes were to be had that included this commemorative music. Some of it was used for training days in New England, but apart from the practical purpose of providing rhythms for marching feet the fife became an instrument of the humble popular virtuoso who played his small instrument in taverns or at fairs or other gatherings as a violin or flute might be played.

Most of this music was homespun, and the songs were quickly improvised, yet their verses—particularly those addressed to Washington—had warmth and immediacy of feeling. None of the music survived after 1825, with the exception of the perennial "Yankee Doodle" and an early Washington march which became the accompaniment for "Hail Columbia." Except for Francis Hopkinson, who dedicated his *Seven Songs for the Harpsichord* to Washington and who may have written one of the marches, the composers, for the most part, were obscure. John Adams considered Hopkinson an oddity yet "genteel and well bred, and very social . . . one of your pretty, little, curious, ingenious men." He had come of a Philadelphia family whose love of music was strong, and he laid public claim, in the preface to the *Songs,* to "being the first native of the United States who has produced a musical composition." Versatile, with a turn for verse-making, Hopkinson also wrote the libretto and music for *The Temple of Minerva,* produced in 1781, which has been considered the first American opera. More strictly, it was an "oratorical entertainment," for it lacked a plot and was distinguished by declamatory musical speeches on a political theme, the American alliance with France. This piece was privately performed in the presence of Washington, Mrs. Washington and the Minister of France. Indeed, though Hopkinson must be counted as one of the first figures in American music, his work was mainly a private venture. *The Temple of Minerva,* in a strict sense an "occasional" piece, never attained a public performance. The harpsichord, for which his *Seven Songs* were composed, was a highly personal instrument and for the drawing-room—

> Come, fair Rosina, come away,
> My generous heart disdains
> The slave of love to be.
> The traveler benighted and lost
> O'er the mountains pursues his lone way
> Beneath a weeping willow shade.

The lines and the music have an unconstrained fluency, as has the lovely title he gave as a young man to a song by Parnell for which he composed an accompaniment, "My Days Have Been So Wondrous Free."

An easy charm characterized Hopkinson's music rather than vigor. In music, as often in his essays, he was a *dilettante.* He had a considerable gift for painting; he was something of an inventor, and the readiness with which he entered upon these diversions suggests the liberality of life in Philadelphia in the era preceding the

Revolution and that immediately following. It was out-side these diversions altogether that Hopkinson's strength lay, in his uncompromising, satirical pamphleteering on behalf of the Revolutionary forces. He was a signer of the Declaration of Independence, and he assumed many governmental responsibilities during the war. He was a personal friend of Franklin, Washington, Jefferson, and when the Revolution was over held high office.

Music for Hopkinson was a personal pleasure, a private luxury; and the music which arose so buoyantly at the close of the Revolution was noticeably social, public, often popular. Concerts had frequently been given in the larger cities before the Revolution, but they had been mainly intimate affairs arranged for small circles of the well-to-do, such as that to which Hopkinson belonged in Philadelphia or the rich merchants in Boston or southern planters in Williamsburg and Charleston. Now large au-diences were enjoying what the Federal *Gazette* called "deep and copious drafts of pure and intellectual pleasure at public concerts," though this pleasure might often be mixed with elements not strictly of the mind. Public con-certs were often given *al fresco* with accompanying fire-works. In Harrowgate, outside Philadelphia, outdoor con-certs were given for some six years from 1790 amid arbors, summer-houses which had rooms for private parties, near mineral springs with facilities for baths and with a plen-tiful supply of liquors. In Savannah in 1796 a "grand con-cert" began with Bach and ended with a hornpipe.

Studious foreign travelers, who clearly expected to find
solemnity or exhaustion in the new nation, tried to explain
the marked phenomenon by another bit of reasoning
when the rousing force of martial music seemed not entirely to account for it. French influence in America, they
said, had brought it about, and indeed this influence undoubtedly played a part in early American musical life.
In Charleston a small group of French musicians became
an enlivening force within the St. Cecilia Society, creating
two orchestras and a chorus; they gave concerts at taverns
as well as before the Society, taught music, copied it for
those who wished to extend their repertoire, and produced ballets and ballet-pantomimes. Elsewhere, in Baltimore, Philadelphia, New York, New Orleans, this influence firmly spread to culminating productions of opera,
some of it continuously over a period of years. When,
after the revolutionary upheavals in France and Santo
Domingo, émigrés began to pour in, many of them turned
their musical aptitudes to account and taught singing,
dancing, the mastery of the flute or violin. Naturally they
gravitated toward those communities in which French
groups had already settled, and these were widely scattered from southern towns to the larger Atlantic cities and
over the Alleghanies to Pittsburgh, Lexington, Louisville,
Ste. Genevieve, St. Louis, New Orleans. To many a small
frontier village they brought a touch of elegance. A fairly
prolific body of dance music appeared with such French

composers as Duport and Capron in the lead. Some of these settled permanently in the larger cities.

The English musicians began to arrive about 1790, and those who in all ways threw themselves whole-heartedly into the American cause probably had a wider popular influence than the French groups. They became associated over a long period of time with the theater, the ballad opera and "oratorical entertainments" and with religious music as organists. Alexander Reinagle, Raynor Taylor, Benjamin Carr, James Hewitt were prime sources of new music for new popular undertakings; some of them wrote the patriotic songs and marches greatly in vogue. None of them was truly distinguished, for English music in this period was at a low ebb; indeed it was because of English indifference to music in this era that these musicians came to America. Adventurous, gay, belonging largely to the theater, they possessed versatility and fluency. Carr was a favorite ballad-singer. He had an operatic career, and he was an organist, pianist and concert-manager; he composed the music for Dunlap's opera based on the William Tell story, *The Archers,* and he established Philadelphia's first music-store, The Musical Repository, with a later branch in New York. Carr also became a publisher of music and founded a musical magazine, the *Musical Miscellany,* which was followed by his *Musical Journal for the Pianoforte,* both of them albums of old and new music; and he was later a leading spirit of the famous Musical Fund Society in Philadelphia.

New societies for the study, patronage and performance of music quickly became a feature of social life in
American cities with a more general membership than
had characterized the musical groups before the Revolution. One of the first of the new organizations was the
Apollonian Society, formed in Pittsburgh about 1800,
which within a few years was offering the music of
Haydn, Pleyel, Bach, Mozart, Handel. Indeed the musical
life of Pittsburgh from at least 1786 provides an index for
the growth of musical sophistication in this period. At the
gateway to the West, with broadhorns crowding the rivers, with chimneys already smoky from the growth of
factories, where all seemed bustle, transitory movement
and commercial activity, music played a noticeable part.
Concerts by traveling musicians were fairly frequent.
Music teachers gravitated to Pittsburgh in considerable
numbers, with French dancing-masters and even a composer, the Irish Dennis Longberry, who not only boasted
of his talents but proved them by furnishing new music
for patriotic occasions.

In all these enterprises foreign musicians played a considerable part. The German-born but English-trained Jo-
hann Christian Graupner had a large share in the music
of the early theater in Boston and established there the
first American orchestra in 1810. Five years later he became one of the founders of the Handel and Haydn Society, which has continued to this day. These musicians
were a positive force in the sudden outflowering of music

after the Revolution. They had both initiative and liberality; they introduced admirable music, new and old, from abroad and responded generously to native tastes. They fostered not only the play with music and the opera but the oratorio, which, with its declamatory aspects, quickly became a favorite American form. Yet to say that they created this musical insurgence or laid a new broad base for American music is to overlook other significant factors. Just as foreign plays were in some measure broadened, simplified, enlivened by American production, so the work of these composers was shaped in part by popular demand. Reinagle's piano sonatas languished; personal, individual music, the music of lyricism or temperament had but a small place. This was as true of Hopkinson's songs as of Reinagle's sonatas. Many such small pieces, with engraved music, appeared in the literary magazines of the day, suggesting the variety and persistence of musical interest; but these magazines, almost as much as in the period of *The Spectator,* represented the patronage of the few. The works, both musical and literary, which they published were mainly those of the *dilettante.* The strong drift of public taste lay in other directions: substantially in music it was practical. The march, the fife tune, music to float a story in a play, opera or ballad, to give breadth and persuasion to religious conviction: these popular uses of music dominated the era.

In these directions the first initiative came from native composers, musicians and printers. In 1785 Isaiah Thomas

advertised music printing from type, and the following
year he issued his successful *Worcester Collection.* Our
first musical journal, *The American Musical Magazine,*
was published in New Haven in 1786 by Amos Doolittle,
known for his engravings of the Battle of Lexington, and
by Daniel Read, a provincial composer. This periodical,
a monthly, continued for a year, and, though its pieces
were mainly homely and religious, it waywardly included
a few of some elegance: a minuet, a plaintive love-song
and two or three pastoral songs that were far from
homely, that were indeed mock-agricultural. A considerable number of American composers had appeared, rude
but vigorous, mainly religious in their themes, whose work
had become popular even before the Revolution: the
principal figure was the Boston tanner, William Billings,
many of whose works had been published. Small pocket
song-books containing their songs and those of others like
them now coming into prominence were constantly being
printed, *The American Harmony* by Oliver Holden, *The
Massachusetts Compiler,* in which Holden had a share,
The Rural Harmony of Joseph Kimball. A long succession
of cheap popular "harmonists" or "songsters" was beginning, which were soon to include secular songs. Nor did
these small volumes provide the only means of preserving
or transmitting music in literate form: a great amount
of individual copying went on regardless of copyrights.
Families traveling into the West carried manuscript
music-books with them, to whose airs and words they

would add as new music became available to them, after the fashion of a diary.

A brief clash in the year 1787 between Andrew Adgate and the French orchestra leader Alexander Juhan in Philadelphia suggests the divergent forces at work and their breadth. Juhan was probably the son of James Juhan, a French musician who had come to Charleston in 1771, had taught music there, and some fifteen years later was in Philadelphia announcing himself speciously as the inventor of the piano. In Charleston his son or brother Alexander had sold a book of his own songs by subscription, as well as *A Set of Six Sonatas* of his own composition. Both the Juhans seem to have been musicians of some knowledge and talent, with a taste for the more delicate forms of music and a liking for private audiences. Alexander Juhan, fussy, pompous, something of a snob, joined in Philadelphia with Reinagle and other English musicians who had founded a series of excellent City Concerts. These were continued successfully through the stormy period in which the Revolution ended and the nation was established, from 1786 to 1794, thus through Washington's first administration. Similar series of subscription concerts were held in Baltimore and in New York. This movement, beginning with energy in the midst of social change and even threatened chaos, was in all ways significant. It placed Americans fairly well abreast of European musical life in this era; and by using the phrase "City Concerts" these musicians had staked out democratic territory, at least in name. They were supported by public subscription, unlike the private subscriptions of the concerts in the larger cities of the colonial period. A somewhat lyrical note in the *Federal Gazette* at the end of 1792 suggests that the democratic intention was explicit: "One bench supports you and one joy unites—there is no struggle for precedency or for place." In a further comment, as he sought to prescribe the kind of music desirable for such gatherings, the writer was on more precarious ground: "In such situations, the music should be smooth and affecting, the songs artless and rural, borrowed chiefly from scenes of country, so the rich man may feel a species of delight in transporting himself a moment from the splendors that usually surround him, to scenes of tranquil and unambitious ease; and the poor man consoles himself to think that some of the most flattering views of life are to be drawn from the situation of those who, like himself, are treading only the humbler walks of life." These pseudo-democratic sentiments were borrowed of course from that poetry and music of the eighteenth century which made agricultural life a dainty pastoral masquerade. But even though this music was both pseudo-democratic and pseudo-agricultural, it must not be discounted; it had a graceful charm, even a light idealism. It caught the American fancy and was to run a considerable course in poetry, drama, opera and song.

Andrew Adgate, with whom Juhan came into conflict, represented music of another order altogether, native in origin, primitive in character, rural in its main sources and mainly religious, though not wholly so, in theme. Little is known of Adgate. He may have been a mechanic; almost certainly he came of humble origins. Little is known, that is, except the bold outlines of his social plans for music. First, in 1784, he opened a school for the encouragement of church music, whose "public singings" became a feature in Philadelphia and whose scope had fresh implications since they were free to all denominations, thus tending to break down theological barriers. This institution was quickly enlarged the following year with the purpose of diffusing a knowledge of music among all classes, particularly the poor. In 1786 Adgate projected a great choral concert with singers drawn from all sections of Philadelphia society. It was this ambitious undertaking that caused the war of words between Adgate and Juhan, who publicly looked down his nose at such efforts and accused Adgate of having "little knowledge of theory," indeed of being confined in the practice of music to the humble practice of "solfa," that is, to the simple antique modes with gapped scales now more generally known as "fasola." An ancient survival, this music had firm root in many parts of the country, particularly among artisans, mechanics, farmers, in rural districts or small towns and villages. Within the period of the Revolution, "solfa" had moved out of oral tradition into the composed music of such lively rude composers as Billings, who used this mode in part. Adgate was including the anthems and "fuges" of Billings in his programs.

The outcome may be surmised. On the one side, was the simple Adgate with a noble, grandiose scheme far in advance of his time, it would seem, as a democratic experiment, which he launched in the chaotic interval following the Revolution. The Constitution had not yet been drafted; indeed up to the Revolution of 1800 anti-democratic forces were strongly to the fore. This was the period of Shays's Rebellion, which made many an American patriot shudder as he considered the possibilities of a rising popular power. Adgate's scheme might have been expected to fail, as one might have expected the triumph of Juhan, whose associations were with established musicians and with men of wealth and position. But the outcome of Juhan's scheme had an unexpected breadth, and Adgate had a great success. Juhan's "City Concerts" continued for many years; and if the enterprise was less truly civic than the name implies, sometimes words stake out large territory that later may be fully occupied. Adgate triumphed also. The great concert that occasioned Juhan's attack upon him was held at the German Reformed Church. For it he assembled a trained chorus of two hundred and thirty voices with some fifty band players, and he included not only the works of the American composers Billings and Tucker but the "Hallelujah Chorus" from Handel's *Messiah*. Francis Hopkinson, whose taste for elegance in music was unmistakable, supported Adgate in these undertakings, as did Benjamin Rush and other distinguished Philadelphians. The press stood with Adgate in his controversy with Juhan and in his public undertakings. His educational projects positively flourished: his Free School became the Uranian Society, then the Uranian Academy. If these transitions involved some curtailment of his original broad plan, his ideas flowed forth in his remarkably successful books. Designed as texts for teaching music to choral groups, his *Rudiments of Music* and his *Philadelphia Harmony* ran through eight editions between 1788 and 1803, and his *Selection of Sacred Harmony* enjoyed a similar popularity.

In his plan for the Uranian Academy, Adgate urged the importance of music in every scheme of education. In this he probably anticipated a similar idea of Noah Webster, who was engaged at this time in an ambitious flurry of lectures in Philadelphia on nationalism in language and literature. Webster announced to his publishers that he was "just beginning to make a bustle . . . and supporting the honor of New England. Even the Philadelphians, who are much inclined to find fault, acknowledge that my remarks are new and my design laudable." Webster had only recently come from Baltimore, where he had taught vocal music by what he called "a regular scientific method," which he offered "in as great perfection as it is taught in America." As to payment, he had been practical, accepting gloves, shoes, slippers and silk stockings in barter for his instruction. In Philadelphia

he met Adgate, who tested his voice and who probably
concurred in the judgment of other Philadelphians that it
was high and nasal with Yankee intonations. Moreover,
Adgate's chorus sang at Webster's lectures. Whether or
not Webster's ideas as to the place of music were derived
from Adgate, or the other way round, they were part of
the flood of ideas and proposals seething in Philadelphia
at this time. Tom Paine was there, exhibiting a model of
an iron bridge, and Webster met him, as he also met
David Rittenhouse, Benjamin Rush and others of the
group who were actively concerned with the rising affairs
of the nation and, in their separate ways, with the sciences and arts. Adgate's plan for the Uranian Society was
published five days after the Constitutional Convention
first assembled.

Adgate's ideas were a little prim, though ingratiating.
Whether or not he was the Absolom Aimwell with whom
he has been identified—the compiler of *The Philadelphia
Songster*—he would have agreed with this worthy as to
what the songs he taught could accomplish: they were
"calculated to please the ear, while they improve the
mind, and make the heart better." His social purposes
were somewhat narrowed as time went on, no doubt by
practical exigencies: his Uranian Society lacked the social
breadth of his original concept and became a somewhat
selective group. The wonder was that this concept, so
essentially democratic, was formulated at all. It preceded
the full formulation of democratic ideas in government.

Two years were to elapse before the national government was fully established, and then its course in democratic practice was hardly charted but was to run through the troubled years during which the Alien and Sedition laws were passed and enforced, up to the Revolution of 1800.

All these nascent ideas were imperfect, but we notice that they appeared in music as well as in political philosophy, and that through music they were attaining tangible forms. Adgate died in 1793 of yellow fever in the epidemic which seemed to single out promising figures in the arts. But his ideas were to continue in diverse forms, nor were they the sudden coruscations of an unknown individual. Like their counterparts in American political philosophy, they had had their antecedents, which have been as largely neglected in approaches to our music as much of the ensuing flow of American music of the pattern outlined by Adgate. This has dropped from view in part because of the persistent notion that the Puritans suppressed music, as they are supposed to have suppressed the other arts, and also because this music was neither great nor always enduring: no great names belong to it. Yet its stream was broad, it had its own color, its own persuasive social design. It still forms a broad underground stream.

2

William Billings was as much a force in the democratic upheaval as were the instigators of Shays's Rebellion. In his own character and person, by the nature and the inverted success of his career he represented a similar populism in music. He came from a class not unallied to that of the embattled farmers, and it was no accident that he became a friend of the leading figure of the new democracy in Boston, Samuel Adams. He was an artisan of Boston, a tanner who used to chalk out tunes on the hides hanging in his shop, a picturesque yet not attractive figure, blind in one eye, with a withered arm, legs of uneven length and a loud voice which he insisted must be heard. In music as in other matters he was self-taught, and he said that rules distracted him: indeed no one could have broken them more freely, even those which represented the most elementary grammar of music. Throughout his life he was ridiculed by boys in the street; with a large family he was always impoverished, though he was well enough thought of in musical circles to command benefits. Before he was twenty-five he had given up tanning for music and become the first American composer—so far as we now know—to make music his profession. If he died in poverty, he had obtained an abundant recognition. The immediate acceptance of his *New England Psalm Singer,* published in 1770, was followed by a warm recognition of his later books. His innovations were widely accepted. If they were also disparaged and even fought, the ensuing warfare only proved their vitality.

Throughout his comparatively short career, Billings carried on a public conversation about his work, mainly by means of the prefaces to his successive hymn-books. He declared his tunes to be "twenty times as powerful as the old slow tunes." Instead of the unison of the old psalms, he offered in his "fuges" the joys of conflict, "each part striving for mastery and victory, the audience entertained and delighted, their minds surpassingly agitated and extremely fluctuated, sometimes declaring for one part, and sometimes for another. Now the solemn bass demands their attention, next the manly tenor; now the lofty counter, now the volatile treble. Now here, now there; now here again,—O ecstatic! Rush on, you sons of harmony!" He confessed that he thought this book "a most masterly and inimitable performance. Oh! how did my foolish heart throb and beat with tumultuous joy," while it was in press. He could hardly wait, he said, until the sheets were stitched and the cover put on, and, when at last the complete book emerged, he cried, "Go forth, my little book, go forth and immortalize the name of your Author; may your sale be rapid and may you speedily run through ten thousand editions, may you be a welcome guest in all companies, and what will add tenfold

to thy dignity, may you find your way into the Libraries
of the Learned."

Later he turned against this book, "his Reuben," as he
had called it. He candidly said it was as "unstable as
water, it did not excel. After impartial examination I have
discovered that many pieces were neither worth my printing nor your inspection"—you being the public. So he selected and corrected the tunes he now most approved of
and added others. But, if he was humble at this point, he
went forth to battle on the major issue. The conflict of
voices that filled him with such jubilation had been called
nothing but jargon by a sober-minded ministry. But he
contended that his tunes, if anything, failed to offer sufficient discord, and to show what might be done in that
direction he composed a tune called "Jargon," whose
words began—

> Let horrid jargon split the air,
> And rive the nerves asunder.

He gave full directions for producing the piece: "Let an
ass bray the bass, let the filing of a saw carry the tenor,
let a hog who is extremely weak squeal the counter, and
let a cart-wheel, which is heavy loaded, and has long
been without grease, squeak the treble; and if the concert
should be too feeble you may add the cracking of a crow,
the howling of a dog, the squalling of a cat, and what
would grace the concert yet more, would be the rubbing
of a wet finger upon the window glass . . . and if all

these in conjunction should not reach the cause,—'accomplish the desired result'—you may add this most inharmonious of all sounds, 'Pay me what thou owest.' "

Billings, in other words, was a composer who lacked nothing in courage and ingenuity. He was a verse-maker in his own right. Not only were the words of "Chester," a favorite during the Revolution and for decades afterward, his own, but he wrote many of the verses for his published musical works, both religious and secular. The opening lines of a choral piece called *Modern Music* have a confident fluency and dash—

> We are met for a concert of modern invention.
> To tickle the ear is our present intention.

For his last book, *The Continental Harmony,* published in 1794, he devised a frontispiece to illustrate his theory of music. It showed a tune with the accompanying words engraved in concentric circles, which was meant to prove that "every tune is a compleat and unbroken circle and that what may be deficient in the first barr is supplied in the last," and that praise should "eternally go round." Above were secular cupids who held a floating banner above the circles, below were musical instruments and music books. With the pedagogical instinct that seemed to be growing in the land, Billings included in this volume a preface in which instruction in the rudiments of music was offered by means of a dialogue.

The boisterous spirit of William Billings pushed its way

into more than one phase of musical life in New England. The cello gave richness to church music as a result of his efforts. In spite of all that has been said about the rude solemnity of New England psalm-singing, it had been possible for the opening bars of a tune to wander off in several directions for lack of pitch. Billings, single-handed, introduced the pitch-pipe into general use. Still a teacher of singing schools, he trained group after group in Boston and in neighboring towns, and drew from them to establish church choirs. The singing society, a more stable affair than the singing school, which he organized in 1786, had a continuous life and is still in existence. But it was his music that spread most widely and had the largest influence. With all their rude joinery, his songs were affirmative, joyous, full of praise, strongly rhythmic, easily memorized. As church music they were novel, but the secret of their wide acceptance lay deeper than this novelty. They arose when the close spiritual identities that had produced the concentrations of unison were going or had gone. Unison in song may, indeed, have outlasted unity of feeling: it would be difficult to say which was altered first. Habit in singing may have outlasted conviction, or, on the contrary, a slow insurgence of new emotion may have first found in music its early instinctive expression. In Billings' music there was little or no sign of a theology, only a sharp break from a form of religious praise which may be called theocratic. This had been completely in the hands of the ministry: it flowed in a single unbroken pattern. Now, with Billings and with others of the same persuasion who quickly followed him this pattern was broken; it fell into lively differences and balances. The singers began and ended together, but, after the first brief musical statement, the different groups of voices entered at successive measures. The basses or counters or tenors might loudly drone or hum through various passages: they created other individual divergences, and the struggle, which now seems crude and comical, undoubtedly produced an exhilarating sense of initiative and independence.

The attacks of the clergy show us how daring was this new phase in religious music, and they were also a partial revelation of the broader musical life of the time. "A catch, a glee, a dance, a march, a common ballad is very improper for the worship of the Most High," said John Hubbard of Dartmouth in 1807. "They have stolen the prostituted air, and with sacrilegious hands have offered it in the Temple of Jehovah." Unexpectedly, religious song had gone back to its prime source, the dance, or to forms that derive from the dance. As the eighteenth century had grown older and luxury had increased, dancing-masters had become increasingly acceptable in Boston; and the tunes used for the slow and stately measures of the day were mainly folk-tunes. But the prime source for Billings as for his fellow-composers would seem to have been the inherited store of balladry which we have been inclined to call Elizabethan but which often included

songs of later lineage. Ballads had been less freely accepted as a portion of early New England life than of life
in the South, partly because of the rise of urban life in
New England and the greater dispersal through migration. The ballads have seemed a less conspicuous heritage
than in the South. But now, in the later eighteenth and
in the early nineteenth century, this heritage was fully
known and accepted. An evidence of this was the readiness with which the "fuges" became popular. Billings
alone, indeed no group of musicians, could so readily
have imposed a radical change upon a place and a period
except by a direct use of familiar musical materials. With
the cloak of Calvinism the colored web of English and
Scotch balladry had been freely worn, and indeed this
circumstance is confirmed by the continuous discovery of
versions of ballads in the rural parts of New England,
particularly in the more northern states, which, like others
from the South, are so old as to indicate that they came
with the first settlers. The adaptations that Billings made
in the basic tunes may sometimes have been slight. But,
as John Powell has pointed out in a similar connection, it
is only in recent times that a distinction has been sharply
drawn between melodic or thematic material already in
existence and that created by the individual. The composer in an earlier day was often literally one who only
put a piece together. Billings did more than this. He
made his own adaptations for the "fuges," and even for
these it seems he sometimes originated tunes. His odes

and anthems cannot have been merely a matter of joinery, for they were repeatedly sung in Boston and Philadelphia in concerts that included music of Haydn and Mozart and less known but sufficiently schooled Europeans. His "Easter Anthem" and his "Rose of Sharon" were favorites from the time of their publication.

Billings earned the full name of composer. He should have it even on the lesser ground, for leading off in a major musical movement by which the buoyancy of the catch, the glee, the ballad was transmuted into praise that broke through the older formalisms. He was a figure in a major movement, which was social, political, religious, economic—where the main stress lay may not easily be determined. Like Billings himself, we may say, "Now here, now there." This movement meant, in matters of the church, an insurgence of the congregation, which theoretically was in power within the Presbyterian and Congregational form, but was not truly so: it meant, in other words, a phase of the breakdown of a dark and rigid dogma and a few stones pulled out from the edifice known as the Standing Order, that clerical organization which stood not only for the old theocracy but pretty consistently upheld all the conservative forces in the community. The striking circumstance is that this alteration was accomplished within the strict fold of Calvinism, not by an insurgent Wesleyism; and the change was consistently democratic. Billings, as we have seen, was a tanner. Oliver Holden of Charlestown, whose *American Harmony* was published in 1792, followed the trade of carpenter until he became a teacher of singing schools. His "Coronation" was to outlast Billings' "Chester," and is still widely sung. Holden planned to establish a paper to be called *The Massachusetts Musical Magazine,* which was intended mainly to offer a repertory for singing schools, with the special attraction of including "principally American compositions." The project fell through, but significantly the emphasis was upon social singing in the schools and upon homespun music.

Social singing became a fever, a passion: the schools burgeoned in towns and hamlets and country places. Jacob Kimball deserted the legal profession to become a teacher and composer, lured perhaps by the considerable sales of the song-books as well as a liking for the life. He died in the almshouse, as a consequence, one must suppose, but not before he had compiled a *Rural Harmony,* particularly intended for country folk. Like most of the other books, it contained an essay on "the principles of music." With all their incidental diversions, the singing schools were truly studious affairs: their object was to *teach,* to induce musical literacy, a sufficient problem, since many of those attending had at best only an elementary knowledge of reading and writing. Many of them came from a class whose life lay not only outside the schools but outside the churches. Even in New England the proportion of the population not affiliated with any church remained large. Yet most of those attending the singing schools evidently favored religious music, since this remained the staple of the books, and they wished not only to sing it but to read it.

The hard struggle was with musical notation, and varied efforts were made to simplify the system. The method which attained an unparalleled popularity was that of the so-called shape-notes, a system by which musical notes were represented by a diamond, a square, a triangle, a circle, with other geometrical shapes that were added decades later when this music moved into the diatonic scale. The invention is ascribed to Andrew Law, a Connecticut clergyman who had also been a singing-master, or to a pair of collaborators, Little and Smith, whose first volume of music with shape-notes, *The Easy Instructor*, was copyrighted in 1802 and may have been published as early as 1798.

The origin of the pair is unknown: their book was published in Philadelphia. Law also lived in Philadelphia and was recommended by the Presbytery there to preach in the South. It seems possible that these several workers in the new field gained something from German musicians. The Mennonites had shunned the established musical notation as a work of popery and the devil, but they promptly adopted shape-notes, and may even have invented them. Law's radical move in giving the melody to the soprano rather than the tenor, which has been thought to come from English psalmists of the period, may well have come from the Germans, who had used the arrangement for two centuries. Shape-notes or "patent notes," as they are still called, at once became immensely popular, the more so since they fell in with a widespread emotional urgency. The Great Revival began in the West in 1800. Within a few years it had spread like an underground fire into many of the smallest hamlets in the eastern states, not as an upflare of a few months but as a continuing agitation of a number of years. Indeed, the wild outbreak on the Red River in Kentucky seems to have set free emotional aptitudes which were to be expressed almost as a ritual, particularly among country people, as a natural form of their religious life. The original impetus came from the traveling Methodist preachers and elders, who, with Bishop Asbury as their leader, had been stirring the embers left by the Great Awakening since 1770. In the West the other sects were quickly aroused, the Presbyterians as well as the Baptists: the sweep of agitation became general. Music freely belonged to it. The Methodist initiative made this inevitable, and for a time small pamphlets containing only the words of hymns were circulated at camp-meetings. Then when the shape-notes solved the problem of a simple musical literacy, the flow of new books that used them began.

So far as is now known, the first of these to appear was compiled by a Vermonter, Joseph Ingalls, and published in Exeter, New Hampshire, in 1805, *The Christian Harmony*. It is not now known whether this little book was immediately related to revivalism or whether it indicated only a simple continuance of the work of the singing schools. Others of the same order may have been published in New England, and these may yet come to light. But shape-note singing was continuously associated with primitive musical modes and primitive or even ancient melodies. It seems not to have taken firm root in New England, perhaps because this region lacked the emotional associations of a strong revivalism—New England was never so deeply swept by the Great Revival as was the West or the South; or perhaps because literacy in all its forms was almost a moral agency in New England communities, and literacy in music was firmly linked with the more difficult modern notation and the diatonic scale. The difference was not merely one of notes: it was emotional. The use of the Ionian, Aeolian, Dorian, Mixolydian modes, in other words of gapped scales utilizing four, five or six notes with added tones which to the modern ear may seem arbitrarily raised or lowered, instead of the full complement of the diatonic, means simply another order of music, with a simpler, a more direct, indeed its own emotional content. The fact that it is primitive means more than that it is old: it has the primitive emotional approach. It was used in England long before the sixteenth century, which means that it belonged to an order of feeling antedating the complexly intellectual religious thought belonging to the Puritans; and this may be the true reason why, even with the lead of Billings, even with the inheritance of ballads and glees and catches cast in these older forms, shape-note religious song, which for many years used mainly the pentatonic or hexatonic scale, did not take firm root in New England. Literacy, complexity, even subtlety prevailed: the modern scale and the modern notation were gradually accepted even in the more remote New England singing schools.

The broad stream of shape-note singing spread through the South, where it was sustained by the country people —"rurals," as they are called by George Pullen Jackson, who first brought their history in that region to light. Its development there forms something more than an episode: it provides a key to broad continuances in regional character. By mischance, music in the South and in the old Southwest has been associated only with the highlands. The implication is that the purer strains have been preserved there by poor and unlettered mountain people who for generations have lived away from the main tides of migration. This conception mingles with another, that the music they have retained is mainly secular. But others living prosperously in the fertile valleys have likewise retained the older modes in music; and these modes are by no means utilized only for the older English and Scottish ballads. In sheer numbers, the religious songs which became deeply traditional with the introduction of shape-notes greatly out-balance flytings and ballads. These have received the greater attention because the interest in balladry, as in other folklore, happened to antedate the interest in religious music. The reasons for this need not detain us here, but the emphasis of the great Child collection of English and Scottish ballads undoubtedly had much to do with it. Sharp was concerned with music, as have been other collectors in the South, but the verbal beauty and interest of the ballads aroused an inevitable concern, particularly when the scholastic hunt for variant lines began. The tendency of modern literary and social criticism to shy away from religious themes and to under-stress religious problems may have been a further influence in this direction. The fact that balladry came down by oral tradition while the religious music was drawn from books may also have made the religious songs seem a less worthy subject for study. In any event, Sharp and most of the collectors who followed in his wake scarcely noticed them: yet they remain highly significant on all counts, embodying deeply striated forces within the national character and offering as well sheer beauty and a seminal influence that has not yet been exhausted.

The transit of shape-notes from Philadelphia to the Valley of Virginia was simple enough, since the roads to and fro had been well marked by migration and commerce even before the Revolution. The German influence may well have been a factor, since the Mennonites, groups of whom had settled in the Valley, adopted the "patent notes" early. The second known volume from this region —and others of the same sort may well have preceded it— was by the Mennonite farmer Joseph Funk, whose *Choral Music,* in German, was compiled at his home in Mountain

Valley and printed at nearby Harrisonburg, in 1816.
Later, when his book appeared in a revised form in English, nearly thirty thousand copies were sold, and it was
again revised with further success. By that time Father
Funk, as he was called, had become a great local figure,
and his dwelling-place had been rechristened Singer's
Glen. When his first book appeared, the Germans made
up the larger numbers of the population in the Valley,
and their influence must still be counted strong even
when their proportions were diminished by the influx of
Celts—Scotch, Irish, Scotch-Irish and Welsh—from across
the mountains or across the sea. The Germans quickly
adopted the English language, and, since they also often
Anglicized their names, their influence is difficult to trace,
but we know that it cannot have been absent from the
vital body of music which developed, since song was their
substantial and revered possession, and one of the best-
known of the later shape-note compilers, William Hauser,
came from a Moravian family. The German inheritance
must have been in large part primitive, or at least in the
primitive mode, since the Mennonites adopted the first
shape-note volumes so readily. In Funk's volumes one
hymn from his later collection goes back, as Jackson has
shown, to a thirteenth-century tune, the *Ass's Sequence*
or *Orientis Partibus.* Here and there, in other compila-
tions, possible traces of German influence appear like em-
blems out of the past: the mention of the "turtle" in a
hymn, or more often of the dove, is reminiscent surely of

the great *Turtel Taube* of Ephrata and of the Biblical imagery which had been appropriated as a widespread symbol. As it happens, the long title of the *Turtel Taube* contains the word "spiritual" in a sense which was to be broadly applied to these songs: it contained the phrase "spiritual rhymes," that is, rhymes created under the influence of the Holy Spirit—not simply rhymes having to do with otherworldly themes. The word "spiritual" had been consistently used by the primitive German sects in this direct and literal manner: their members had been called "spirituals," and "spirituals" the new songs were finally to be called—no one knows just when the usage began—as expressing what was believed to be their character, that of direct communication with the Holy Spirit, particularly under the influence of the psychic disturbance and release of the revival.

Beneath the strong flow of music which these Germans inevitably brought to the Valley lay the primary fact that they were pietists, whose religion, with its simple rituals of baptism and foot-washing, was essentially primitive. In revivalism and other larger matters they found themselves fairly at one with the Scotch, Scotch-Irish and Welsh whose numbers sharply increased in the Valley at the beginning of the nineteenth century, coming from across the mountains or across the sea. They were Methodists for the most part, or they readily yielded to the sway of traveling Methodist elders or preachers. Music from folk-sources had long been drawn upon for Metho-

dist worship. When Wesley said that he saw no reason
why the devil should have all the pretty tunes, he apparently did not mean that true religionists should compose
pretty tunes of their own, though they were undoubtedly
free to do so, but that they should take the devil's tunes,
particularly the dances, and turn them to religious uses.
In the Great Revival of the West, and now in the smaller
religious gatherings of the same order that were spreading
out in its wake, something resembling a primitive dance
took place, in ecstatic, circling, swinging movements, in
jumping, jerking, stamping and leaping when excitement
rose to a height. In later years, with entire reverence, one
of the most popular of the "fasola" compilers, William
Hauser of Georgia, utilized the "Fisher's Hornpipe" for
a persuasive querying song that began, "Good morning,
brother Pilgrim: what, traveling to Zion?" Through
eleven stanzas he made the Irish jig carry his argument
that the religious dance was justified. These exercises
were defended as being similar to David's dance before
the Ark. Irish fiddle-tunes in triple quick time lent themselves to hosannas. Phrases of "Yankee Doodle," which
almost certainly seems of Irish origin, slipped into a
hymn, linked with other fragments of melody, and praises
were sung to bagpipe-tunes.

Some of the melodies harked back to the middle ages
and may have been religious in origin or in early use,
while many others were adaptations of the more famous
ballads, "Lord Thomas and Fair Eleanor," "Barbara Al-

len," "Lord Lovel" and others that already had had a
varied history in high and low estate. The tunes cannot
be fully traced, yet their folk-origin is clear and their
broad relation to the dance is also plain. A few have a
literary origin or association, like the popular "Romish
Lady," mentioned in *The Knight of the Burning Pestle*,
which describes the catastrophe following "civil mirth"
by a Catholic. Since in one way or another most of the
singers knew the sea, it was inevitable that maritime
songs should be used by them, and, as if some original
emotion still lingered with the air, they were often singu-
larly beautiful.

The Shakers

TO FOUND the single-minded community had been a pronounced impulse in the colonial period. Something more than a wish for freedom of worship had lain behind the concentrations of the Pilgrims, the Puritans, the Quakers in Pennsylvania, the Mennonites, the Dunkers, the Moravians. The word "separatist" which was applied to some of these sects and was to attach itself to others in a later period had a significance beyond that of theology. They were all in some sense separatists, not only in their digression from main stems of belief but in their passionate wish to draw boundaries around themselves as social units. Their intolerances and even the persecutions which some of them inflicted upon other sects perhaps sprang as much from a rude fear of social disintegration as from a theology. With the religious upheavals of the Reformation had come profound social upheavals, which had meant not only political changes throughout northern Europe but severances of many deeply set human ties. The community represented an effort to sustain these ties. Extending them beyond the boundaries of the given church into the realm of social organization produced—as long as the boundaries could endure—a new and almost primitive stability.

These impulses were by no means confined to the period of the early settlements when closely knit communal organizations had special validity in the midst of the wilderness. They were scattered down the decades to the era of the Revolution when other communities coalesced with new vigor and a rising conviction that the Millennium had come. Jemima Wilkinson, the Public Universal Friend, led a band of her followers into an unsettled region of upper New York where they established themselves in 1788 on the shore of Seneca Lake. The communal faith of the Shakers took form during the Revolution; and thereafter a series of communities were founded not only by the Shakers, whose efforts multiplied, but by others, the Rappites of Economy in western Pennsylvania and later of Harmony in Indiana, and the Separatists of Zoar, both of German origin. These were followed by others whose purposes were widely divergent, so many indeed that the impulse toward communal organization formed a conspicuous strain through something like a hundred years of our history. Because many of these experiments failed and none of them became exemplars for wider movements of the same order, and because their numbers were relatively small in the aggregate, they have been regarded for the most part as oddities springing up within the Republic, yet the impulse which created them was almost continuous throughout our history up to, say,

1875. They all occasioned widespread discussion, and, with the exception of the community at New Harmony under the leadership of Robert Owen and the transcendental gathering at Fruitlands, they all developed out of popular movements and even with their limited numbers represented widespread popular concerns. They concentrated essential purposes; even their apparent eccentricities may have something to say as to the social character of their times. The impulse toward social unity is a profound impulse, and possibly these organizations offered something of a challenge to the new republic which so quickly began to spread over the country like a great wild vine.

Of all these new communal organizations, those of the Shakers were among the earliest. They became the most widely spread, they established the most richly integrated culture, and they were the most enduring. In spite of poverty and persecution, they founded some twelve communities in the five years between 1787 and 1792, at New Lebanon, Watervliet and Groveland in New York, Hancock, Tyringham, and Enfield in Connecticut, Harvard and Shirley in Massachusetts, Canterbury and Enfield in New Hampshire, Alfred and New Gloucester in Maine. Some thirteen years later, the foundation of Shaker colonies in Kentucky and Ohio began, with a wider geographic spread and the beginnings of prosperity. Yet in 1780 the original band under Ann Lee had numbered only twelve. Because of their practice of celibacy, they seemed, of all these communities, the least likely to survive, yet their numbers steadily increased, with strong additions as whole families fulfilled the rigorous requirements exacted by the sect and young people learned and furthered its beliefs and traditions. No other community created and sustained its own modes in music, the crafts, and even in architecture as did the Shakers or established so individual a way of life.

Set apart from the world by conviction, they seemed unworldly in character as individuals and as a sect, yet they became prosperous, and, as by clairvoyance, reflected major movements within the country, continually passing into new phases that mirrored dominant concerns —intellectual, emotional, social, practical—outside their own communities. Sometimes in major preoccupations they seemed an advance guard. In trade and in the crafts, they set extraordinarily high standards, just as in ways of belief and of living they maintained strange divergencies from what we regard as the norm. Above all the Shakers were expressive, not only through their beliefs or "orders," but in their crafts, their music, their dancing, their rituals and their writing. The turn toward autobiography which had been marked in our colonial life was continued by the Shakers in personal "testimonies" that multiplied down the years. Many of these were assembled and published; numbers still exist in manuscript. Their covenants were written and continually revised; they kept written records of community life that were not intended for publication yet gave rein to literary expression. Their history, their beliefs led to an extensive printed literature of great dignity and sometimes of poetic quality. Inevitably they became involved in controversies with individuals and sometimes with local or state governments, with ensuing pamphlets on both sides, with the result that their tenets and mode of life became widely publicized. Many transitory publications relating to the Shakers have undoubtedly disappeared, yet the literature relating to them was large and widespread, increasing in volume at least from 1815. Undoubtedly their tenets of celibacy created a curiosity which made them talked about more freely than were other sects. They themselves were downright in their handling of the question of sex, using in their early period at least uncompromising and earthy language which in turn was employed by many who opposed them. Language relating to the Shakers could always claim vitality. They were not quietist, as were the Quakers from whom they sprang in England, even though they embraced many quietist principles. From the time of their early persecutions in this country they were known, heard, reckoned with. In the language of those revivals which so powerfully shaped their destiny, they were a power.

Their founder was a woman, and equality between the sexes ran through both their practical orders and their spiritual beliefs. With this emphasis came another, upon the worth of common folk. The Shakers were proud of the humble origin of Ann Lee and would speak of the carpenter's son of Judea, the blacksmith's daughter of England. The rise of Shakerism in a region where mechanics and the crafts occupied a dominant place, where the industrial revolution was to begin, undoubtedly had a strong influence upon the worldly preoccupations of the Shakers. Ann Lee, who was unlettered, had worked in a cotton factory and later as a cutter of hatters' fur before her early marriage. Her admonition "Put your hands to work and your hearts to God" was carried through Shaker history. She urged her followers against debt, counseled them to neatness and thrift. "There are no slovens nor sluts in heaven," she said. A young woman who became one of her earliest followers at Watervliet said, "Though I was brought up in New England, among good farmers, I never saw before such neatness and economy as was here displayed in the wilderness."

These astringencies were joined with other, quite different elements, in Ann Lee's character as in her followers. She possessed that gift for psychic elevation or "possession," which in an earlier generation had led to charges of witchcraft among those by whom it was displayed, leading to visions, the laying on of hands or healing, speaking with tongues, and persuasive emotional power.

In Ann Lee, this psychic force seems to have been loosed by an unhappy marriage and perhaps further by the loss of her four children; she had been repelled by the marriage relationship before she entered it. Her repulsion, gathering weight and joining with a sense of purity through conversion, laid the foundation for the belief in celibacy which became a foundation-stone among the Shakers. But Ann Lee's infectious psychic power had other origins. She was born in 1736, when the influence of the French Camisards, considered prophets, was still felt in Lancashire, to which they had migrated some thirty years earlier. The Shakers, who always had a strong sense of history, were aware of this religious ancestry. It figures in their religious chronicles; it was mentioned in one of their early hymns that is half a ballad. Through these dramatic French figures, disruption came to the Quakers, or another form of separatism. The Shaking Quakers or Shakers, who shook to rid themselves of sin, were organized under the Wardleys while Ann was still a girl; it was from them that she first gained religious conviction, though it was some fifteen years before this conviction acquired the dynamic energy which brought her to America and made her the founder of a sect whose tenets were far more complex than those of the Wardleys.

Mother Ann, as she was called by her followers, was "of a strong constitution, rather exceeding the ordinary size of women; very straight and well proportioned in form . . . rather thick . . . very majestic," said one of them. "Many of the world, who saw her without prejudice, called her beautiful." Her hair was chestnut, her eyes blue, her manner mild; she would enter a room sing-

ing and is said to have given the Shakers by revelation
their peculiar mode of musical notation as well as many
of their early tunes which at first were wordless. But with
her mildness went a spirit that was trenchant, even gay.
"Be joyful!" was her command. Her reproofs were sharp
and homely: to a man walking the floor in desperate
travail she exclaimed, "Hold up your head—God made
man upright. Don't lean against walls. You walk crooked.
Be cheerful—be cheerful!" She did not hesitate to level
charges against those who she felt came to her hypo-
critically. "You filthy whore!" she cried to a prurient
woman, apparently on sight. "The devil is a real being,"
she insisted, "as real as a bear. I know, for I have seen
him and fought with him." Her forthright sayings were
preserved in records by her early followers, as was much
of the speech of her brother William—later Father William—who joined in the visionary exodus of the small
band to America and had much the same temper. A
great, strapping, handsome, illiterate man who had once
been an officer in the grenadiers, wearing his long curly
hair free almost to his waist, a fine singer with a flaming
gift for transmitting emotion and conviction, William Lee
could face an accuser with a torrent of bold language;
equally he could lay out a garden in beautiful order, and
one of his songs, composed in the midst of persecutions
in the village of Harvard, was known as "Father William's Dove Song."

The religious experiences of these two culminated in

England with an attack upon the Shaking Quakers by a
mob when Ann began openly to preach against marriage,
with subsequent imprisonment, with further persecutions
and miraculous escapes, all of which as recounted by
these two and the four others who followed them passed
into Shaker lore. Then Ann began to heal the sick and
the injured, though healing never became an integral part
of Shaker hopes or expectations. Sometimes a "gift" of
healing occurred among later Shakers, but this was accepted with that marked equanimity which became part
of the Shaker mode. The constant, increasing form of
religious manifestation was the vision. It was a vision of
Ann Lee in the midst of persecution which led to the
foundation of her millennial church and the Shaker com-
munes in America. "I had a vision of America," she said.
"I saw a large tree, every leaf of which shone with such
brightness as made it appear like a burning torch. . . . I
knew that God had a chosen people in America; I saw
some of them in a vision and when I met with them in
America I knew them. . . ." This was undoubtedly the tree
of life, which, with the crystal stream and other images
from Revelation, was to play so large a part in the Shaker
cosmology. Angels appeared over the masts of the damaged and leaky ship on which the small band traveled to
America in 1774. It was typical that its members should
see them in the midst of a storm and also man the pumps.
The urge of work—or what in another connection was

called "labor"—appeared in their most uplifted moments.
The Shaker meaning of the word "labor" was significant.
To labor was a hard, concentrated effort of mind and
spirit directed toward the solution of inner difficulties and
a final peace.

With Ann and William Lee on this voyage were Ann's
husband, known as Abraham Stanley, who soon left her,
John Hocknell, the only one of the band possessed of
means, James Whitaker, a vigorous youth of unmistakable piety, and a few others. After an interval they went
to Watervliet, then called Niskeyuna, a primitive settlement in the woods a few miles from Albany, where their
teachings began, with the harsh persecutions, mainly by
mobs, which were to dog them on many journeys and
which no doubt led to the early death of Ann and William Lee, as also that of James Whitaker, the first "lead"
of the Shakers to follow them. They had arrived in Niskeyuna shortly before the outbreak of the Revolution;
and, since they preached peace with the doctrine of the
Second Coming, and since they had come from England
themselves, they were suspected of being British spies.
Ann's bold denunciations of the institution of marriage
seemed nothing short of madness, even witchcraft, to the
few country people on a rude frontier. All the members
of the band were imprisoned on a charge of treason, but
they were finally released. No writer has filled in the gaps
in time between the arrival of this group in Niskeyuna

and the journey which they made to Lebanon when they left prison; plainly one strength of the Shaker movement derived from the Baptist revival, begun there the year before, to which they directed themselves, though Ann Lee's leadership became manifest.

The revival—breaking out in the midst of the Revolution—took the usual form, with the coming together of crowds, the sweeping, scourging stress of revivalistic preaching, exhortation and stormy prayer; but it is notable that neither Ann Lee nor any of her followers used this traditional mode, long since established by the Whitefield revival. They spoke, as did those of the sect from which they had sprung, the Quakers, as the spirit moved them. Throughout the brief remainder of her life, Ann Lee seems to have made no attempt to reach crowds; she worked with the few; the familiar picture is of the small group in a room. Whether or not this mode was imposed upon her because her teachings were strange, her followers few, a method was established at variance with that of the revival of crowds, which was to be repeated so frequently throughout the country and through many years. The Shakers were sometimes to draw upon the fruits of the revival, but their modes of conversion and communication remained limited, personal, intensive, made for the great goal of union, which was expressed in the Shaker commune but had in the Shaker philosophy a larger significance.

> 'Tis the union of each other
> That doth make believers strong

said one of the early hymns,

> Be not anxious to go forward,
> And to leave your brother dear;
> You may happen to fall backward,
> And your brother forward stear.

This argument was followed by another as to the charms of spiritual companionship and the difficulties of individual "warfare," but the larger idea was plain: the communal experience was on a higher level than any which the individual alone could achieve. No solitary labors of the soul are recorded by the Shakers except as a prelude to an acceptance to Shaker beliefs: the simplest experiences, even of everyday life, were to be wrought in common. No tasks were done alone: provision was invariably made that two or three or more would work together. "United inheritance" was a basic phrase, a basic belief. The name of the sect, "The United Society of Believers," had a more than formal meaning. The gathering of the church "into one Joint Interest and Union, that all might have an equal right and privilege, according to their calling and needs, in things both Spiritual and Temporal," was the purpose of the First Covenant, drawn up in 1795. Its principles had then been practiced for some years; it was afterwards several times amended to strengthen its legal force.

A body of Shaker belief, taking early shape, marked this sect as, among other things, substantially set against Calvinism. The Shakers rejected the doctrine of the Atonement; they argued publicly against what they called the "horrid and blasphemous doctrines of election and reprobation." They found the doctrine of the resurrection of the body, accepted by many of the new evangelical sects, "repugnant." They employed no sacraments, though they created inspirational ceremonies. Their attack upon the Calvinist acceptance of "eternal and unconditional decrees" gives a clue to a striking element in Shaker thought. Not only did they regard such decrees as "horrid and blasphemous" but they rejected many absolutes altogether. They did not accept the Bible as final truth. "The Evangelists wrote according to the best of their knowledge," or "saw through a glass darkly." The Book of Revelation seemed to them to have suffered least through human transmission, and its imagery as well as its half-pagan, half-daemonic spirit infused much of their thought: they relied at every turn upon revelation, or, as they preferred to call it, inspiration. Yet in their concept of inspiration there was nothing fragmentary, disjointed, disorderly: the Shakers were dominated by an idea inherent in major movements of nineteenth-century thought, the idea of progress. Few words appear in Shaker writings more frequently than the word "travel." The Shakers traveled in thought, they would "travel a song." Sometimes "travel" seemed equivalent to "travail," and indeed "labor" often appeared to mean "travel." To labor, though less peacefully, in the spirit, meant not only the effort to break bonds but to create anew. In the preface to *Millennial Praises,* the first collection of Shaker hymns, published at Hancock in 1813, the anonymous writer makes the principle clear: "It is not to be expected that the people of God will ever be confined in their mode of worship to any particular set of hymns or any other regular system of words—for words are but signs of our ideas, and of course must vary with the increasing work of God. Therefore these compositions, though they may evince to future believers the work and worship of God at this day, yet there can be no rule to direct them in that work of God which may hereafter be required of his people. . . . The work of regeneration is an increasing work . . . a continual travel from grace to grace. . . . Therefore these hymns, wherever they may be sung by Believers, must be limited to the period of their usefulness; for no gift or order of God can be binding on believers for a longer time than can be profitable to their travel in the gospel."

Thus with the idea of progress was interwoven another which has been considered almost contemporary, that of functionalism. These hymns had no absolute value, much less were they thought to have beauty. In the strictest sense they were practical music, devised to induce certain experiences or states of being. They were to be discarded when their usefulness was over. The same idea

was to infuse the Shaker sense of handicrafts, which were
evolved at first from the plain forms of the early frontiers
because economy was essential in the new communities.
The stripping of the objects made—furniture, weaving,
and the like—to what was demanded by mere use was
later followed with closer exactions. Rejection of all ornament quickly became part of the Shaker philosophy,
complementing the stress upon use, not only use in the
crude sense but adaptations for use: there was nothing
set or fixed in the Shaker development of the crafts.

Functionalism, with an acceptance of change, likewise
belonged to their concepts of church government, for
which they devised no written forms. These affairs were
to be determined "according to present circumstances."
The Shakers had no written confession of faith, no creed.
The idea of change was implicit in their underlying concept of spiritual government through revelation. Though
they believed that the Millennium had come—this belief
was indeed the keystone of their faith—the promised
thousand years of peace by no means meant to them a
fixed pattern or state of being: change or "travel" was
constantly to be in view. Even in eternity the Shakers
foresaw no absolutes of experience. Probation was accepted as an intermediate state following death. In a
later period they evolved a belief in great cycles of eternal life. The only absolute was God, and, with a humility
which had not belonged to all other Christian sects, the
Shakers believed that they could never see God. Their

concept of God was close to that which Ethan Allen in Vermont was evolving at about the same time in his "Oracle of Reason": that a concept of God which could be formulated and understood by man was clearly unacceptable, since infinity itself was beyond man's comprehension.

To these ideas, which have so modern a cast, was added another group that has seemed in its simplest form to belong to our own time, relating to equality for women. Undoubtedly its origin lay in the persuasive leadership of Ann Lee. There is no certain evidence that she regarded herself as the second appearance of Christ on earth; as late as 1827 one of her early disciples spoke of her simply as "a woman of God," possessing deep piety, purity, the gifts of prophecy and of healing. Some of the early testimonies and some of the early writings suggest at most that by her gifts and revelations she showed that the Millennium had begun. But the earliest exposition of Shaker beliefs, *Christ's Second Appearing,* written by three of the early disciples, first published at Lebanon, Ohio, in 1808, and several times reprinted, indicated a prevailing or growing conviction by its title and argument and also by a brief and entirely humble notation of the writers by which they likened themselves to the writers of the Gospels. The rejection of a written creed by the Shakers by no means excluded the writing of works on Shaker beliefs. This work, indeed, was published by order of the ministry; it embodied concepts that were

taking form, though by no means final form. By a mi-
nutely detailed argument, springing mainly from references to the Bride in Revelation but developed also from
every other possible Biblical allusion, a whole canon as
to the spiritual position of woman or of the feminine
principle was created. God, according to Shaker teaching, was both masculine and feminine: the appearance
of Jesus and the Second Appearance through Ann were
revelations of that dual nature. The male element in God
was love, the female was wisdom. The writers of *Christ's
Second Appearing* speak tenderly of woman as "the most
glorious part in the creation of man . . . that most ami-
able part." A substantial belief grew up that differences
in sex persisted through all eternity. The Shakers accepted the simple statement of Genesis that woman was
responsible for the fall, nor had they any doubt as to the
nature of the temptation which she had offered: the first
sin was carnal, and they never failed to stress its deprav-
ity. Their belief in celibacy—so passionately defended—
sprang from this conclusion. Yet this logic in no way upset their tenets of equality, which ran consistently through
the Shaker way of life during its entire course, from 1792
when the church was fully established. As eldresses,
women occupied positions entirely equal to that of the
elders. A spirited, handsome, intellectual young woman
from Pittsfield, Lucy Wright, assumed the leadership of
the Society in 1796 after the death of James Whitaker,
then of Joseph Meacham, both leaders who had been

among the first disciples. When Mother Ann first saw Lucy Wright she had exclaimed, "We must have her; she will be worth a whole nation." A born executive, not hasty but with what one of the later sisters called "a vein of cool calculating prudence and discretion," she put order into what was still a hesitant and ill-established organization; no doubt the standing of her family as well as her own serene and dominant character had much to do with the decline of the rougher forms of opposition encountered by the Shakers. Under her guidance, the new strong Shaker societies in the West were formed in 1805. For some twenty-five years, until her death in 1821, when the Shakers had achieved notable prosperity and peace, Lucy Wright remained at the head of the societies, then numbering sixteen. Her husband, Elizur Goodrich, had joined the Shakers when she did and became an elder. It will be noted that she kept her own name.

A line of notable women appeared in Shaker history, highly individualized, possessed of a variety of gifts that flowed into the uses of the Society. Stress upon duality, upon the two, was repeated in both practical and metaphorical terms by the Shakers:

> Two tables did the law complete,
> Two cherubs on the mercy-seat,
> Two silver trumpets plainly shew
> That gospel truth proceeds from two;
> And though the priests one goat did slay,
> The second bore their sins away.

Two olive trees supplied the bowl,
As life from Christ supplies the soul;
And certain as the vision's true,
The male and female are the two.

The Shaker philosophy as to the position of women was formulated some years before Mary Wollstonecraft's treatise and was put into energetic practice. Perhaps the equality of women on the frontier provided a receptive ground for these ideas, but it must be noted that they flourished explicitly only among the Shakers, far in advance of their formulation in this country as a social or political program. Shaker functionalism may likewise have sprung from the frontier pattern of experience, out of which indeed a whole American attitude was developing: if something worked, hold on to it; if not, discard it. Shaker thought reached beyond this to a rude pragmatism. Transmutation into further spiritual states was the Shaker objective. Not whether something worked as an immediacy but whether it produced significant change was the prime consideration. As for the Shaker concept of progress, its sources cannot be easily ascertained. Men and women of education and even of learning joined the sect; more than one early Shaker work used the apparatus of scholarship. Some of these members may have gained the primary idea from reading the French *philosophes* or from current discussion of their works, but, if so, they had employed stout and selective thinking, for the *philosophes* were abhorred by the orthodox in New

England; their names were by-words. When their ideas were accepted, as by rash young men at Yale or Harvard, these had of course been linked with concepts of deism, not those of the Christian faith.

By whatever means the Shakers had seized upon them, they had somehow discovered and accepted early ideas that were to run through a native practical philosophy. They were indeed acutely conscious of an identity with American principles, sometimes naively transmuting these into terms of Revelation. Mother Ann, they said, "flew into the wilderness of America on the wings of Liberty and Independence." They sang in praise of the rights of conscience:

> Rights of conscience in these days,
> Now demand our solemn praise;
> Here we see what God has done,
> By his servant Washington,
> Who with wisdom was endow'd
> By an angel, through the cloud,
> And led forth, in wisdom's plan,
> To secure the rights of man.

An early Shaker definition of the Millennium—1808—was of an era "in which all tyrannical and oppressive governments shall be overthrown and destroyed, and mankind enjoy just and equal rights in all matters, civil and religious." Their earliest covenant spoke of their order as founded on "the generous soil of North America." They referred to the American eagle as "the brightest ensign

of civil and religious liberty ever raised on earth since
the fall of man." The idea of freedom was transformed
into a religious experience, freedom from the bondage of
sin, freedom from the bonds of the world, freedom to
"travel" into farther spiritual states, to attain "the real
work of God that simplifies the soul." One of Mother
Ann's most frequently repeated sayings was "I knew that
God had a chosen people in America," stressing a conviction that had frequently belonged to millenarian sects
and that was to take other, secular forms and was repeated again in the idea of the promised land.

The Shakers were in all senses a native sect not only
because of these convictions but because they were so
firmly rooted here, by so many ties; nor were they the less
so because in so many respects they embodied primitive
elements. Like the New Lights or Campbellites, recently
formed in Kentucky, they hoped to recover the force
and direct truth of the apostolic church, "the primitive
church," which they frequently mentioned. They expected pentecostal gifts and, as they thought, experienced them, through dancing, song, and finally—though
in this period only as a beginning—through visions and
direct communication with the spirit world.

Shaking to throw off evil spirits, dancing to trample
down the natural man, had not only been ridiculed by
many in the "world," but in the early days was sometimes
a subject of doubt on the part of the Shakers themselves.
Josiah Talcott at New Lebanon "labored for a season

under severe buffeting," according to a manuscript record, "relative to dancing." An evil buffeting spirit whis-
pered, "You wear out a great deal of shoe leather dancing
and it does no good." Josiah replied bluntly to the buffeter, "What's that to you? I tan my own leather," and
went on dancing, though he was frequently beset by
doubts. The argument of the buffeter, who seems to have
been Satan himself, had a certain weight. Puncheon floors
were hard on shoes; leather was dear. The Shakers were
said to have learned to tan their own leather for this express reason. Certainly they did not give up dancing:

> Shaking here, and shaking there,
> People shaking everywhere,
> Since I have my sins confessed,
> I can shake among the rest.
>
> We'll be shaken to and fro,
> Till we let old Adam go;
> When our souls are born again
> We unshaken shall remain.
>
> Though the wicked stand and mock
> They shall not escape the shock;
> All the world will have to say
> Shaking is no foolish play.

Another hymn suggests the origin of the violent exercises
by which the Shakers were moved during the revival of
1807:

> Now do we find a great increase,
> While shaking spreads from west to east.

It was two years earlier that three Shaker brothers had gone to the West, having learned of the Kentucky Revival, and had helped to found in Ohio and in Kentucky a substantial number of Shaker communities, which were to grow in power. The extreme physical manifestations of the Great Awakening—the jerks, bending, dancing, even barking like dogs and other physical manifestations —had seemed to the Shakers, as to the new converts there, signs of the descent of the holy spirit; in consequence, many of these motions spread by contagion to the eastern Shakers. The jerks were supposed to humiliate the individual who displayed these abrupt, automatic motions; and for a time the quieter eastern Shakers were beset by them. Sometimes a whole group would have a sudden "gift" to sit on the floor or would lapse freely into what they called "a lively dance."

Undoubtedly under Mother Ann's early ministrations and during outbreaks of the revivalistic spirit in later periods, shaking or dancing among the Shakers sometimes took on violent forms. But the contagion from the West met a powerful counter-check in the character of Lucy Wright, who gave to Shaker dancing an effect of order which it tended to keep even under powerful excitement, teaching believers to subdue irregular and individualistic motions—in other words, inducing them to move in the rhythm that was consistent with the whole doctrine of "union." Lucy Wright taught a symbolic use of the hands that was to develop into a conspicuous part of Shaker ceremonials. Instead of miscellaneous and violent dancing motions, she taught the Shakers in all the eastern communities a kind of double hop or little sliding motion of the foot, and led them to travel—symbolically—in a circle. A downward shaking of the hands to shake out evil was employed instead of a violent shaking of the whole body. The upturned palm signified readiness to receive spiritual gifts with an inward motion to indicate that these gifts were being accepted and stored. Shuffling movements and mathematical formations, marches and counter-marches, with the brethren lined up on one side, the sisters on the other, became typical, with some three or four hundred Shakers sometimes participating as their numbers increased.

Sometimes the dance meant "freedom," that is, liberation into the certainty of spiritual experience, but equally it could mean a transitional rite. "To labor in the square order" meant to join in a communal effort to achieve that experience. Song might be combined with dancing. "We traveled two songs"—in this case traveling was physical as well as spiritual. "Singing refreshed our hungry souls." Speech might interrupt the social dance, as testimony on the part of an inspired brother. Not during a revival but on a Sabbath in 1824, "nearly all the apostolic gifts were revived in the public meeting and in the church—new tongues, new songs, signs, mighty shaking, turning, and divers operations of the mighty power of God."

These were mainly social though not wholly so. Joseph

Meacham, Ann Lee's "first born in America" and the first leader of the Shakers after the death of the original band, had no aptitude for dancing, but he practiced its forms alone until he wore the boards smooth in an attic room, and thereafter "seemed to exercise more like a spirit than a human being." Jemima Blanchard, who had been a spoiled child, a shy girl,—moved at Harvard to defy her family's wishes and to join the Shakers during Ann Lee's sway there,—later became notable for gifts of movement, and "would sometimes go from the Square House to the South House, whirling rapidly and passing over fences or whatever came in her way without touching them or making the least effort to clear them. At times she would be entirely supported by the power without touching any material thing." These statements are taken from Shaker testimonies.

Music played a conspicuous part in Shaker life from the beginning, because both Ann and William Lee accompanied their ministrations by song. After being beaten by the mob at Shirley, "Elder James had a new song of praise put into his mouth," of which two lines were recorded by a form of notation peculiar to the Shakers, said to have been given to Mother Ann by inspiration. The first seven letters of the alphabet were employed, with "a" designating middle C, thence upward through the octave, and with differences in the form of the letters indicating differences in the length of the notes. Thus Roman letters indicated quarter-notes, italics eighth-notes, while half-notes were designated by the addition of single lines beside the letters. Other signs indicated rests or grace-notes, staccato or rubato. This form of notation, one of the several contrived during this period in the effort to make possible the reading of music by the many, was practiced by the Shakers for many years. Much simpler to write than shape-notes, this system lent itself to rapid manuscript records. These were abundant, and from the fluency with which they were obviously written it is clear that the system became a common language, easily understood. The first recorded songs were brief and wordless; others of an early period were set to strange syllables "by the gift of tongues," but though wordless songs—a low humming—were abandoned about 1810, new songs in strange tongues were created by inspiration for many years, recorded, and learned with precision.

Again in the development of song the Great Awakening in the West was a powerful influence. The outbreak of song there had accustomed many individuals to its use. The Western Shakers, accepting these believers, also accepted their abundant mode of song. The custom spread and "brought forth talents" in the East as in the West. Verse-making, so widely spread since the Revolution, combined with the making of tunes; the music of an anthem might be written by one, the words by another. In accord with communal principles the writers were seldom or never mentioned. *Millennial Praises*, pub-

lished without music, and containing some one hundred
and forty religious songs, some of them many stanzas in
length, is an early testimony to the abundant creative
impulse of the Shakers in music, and at the same time a
homely record of their beliefs, experiences and history.
Many of the songs are in truth ballads, telling the story
of Mother Ann, of the "everlasting parents," of the coming of the word to America. The tenderest feelings might
be expressed in them, yet the writers were not above an
occasional pun, as when speaking of the "wine" they
spoke in the same breath of the Lees. Some of the songs
were as simple as was indicated by the title "My Feelings." The devil might be referred to as "the old man."
The stanzaic forms could sometimes be fairly complex,
with shortened verses and internal rhymes. These songs
were typical of an unhesitant outpouring, which was to
continue for more than half a century in extraordinary
volume, remaining unknown because the songs were
rarely printed until a much later date. They were made
familiar by manuscripts and quickly learned by heart.
Many Shakers were said to know as many as a thousand
songs, and they carried songs of greeting to other communities when they made visits and composed songs of
farewell. Songs were sent in letters, and new songs were
constantly composed during extraordinary "manifestations of the spirit."

Symbolic motions of the hands were combined with
songs as well as with shaking and dancing, so that some-

thing like a ritual developed, though nothing occurred in fixed sequences; the operation of the spirit often reversed procedures. These changeable sequences achieved an extraordinary unison, as if a whole society were moved as one, and these unities were heightened in effect by unities in dress. Well into the early nineteenth century, Shaker men wore a costume belonging to an earlier period, long-tailed blue coats, breeches with polished buckles at the knee and on square-toed shoes, but these were finally discarded, in part because indigo was dear and also because a plainer, less pretentious dress accorded better with Shaker principles. At first the costume of an older day may have been preserved to give dignity to a struggling organization, or it may only have been retained longer in the back country than in the towns. In any event it gave way to drab or gray, with long trousers, long coats, drab hats. The women's dress, also gray, was gradually changed to include the severe ascetic bonnet or simple coif with lawn or woolen shoulder capes that became an enduring form of feminine Shaker wear. From the first a tailoring shop had been established at New Lebanon; suitable outer raiment always seemed important to the Shakers, and costumes were made with great precision, as was everything the Shakers touched. The cut of garments, the number of buttons, the size of hats were all prescribed, and though blue for dress was abandoned, the color remained dominant on the Shaker scene, beloved and finally symbolic for the Shakers, a deep astrin-

gent blue based on cobalt, which was to be seen elsewhere in New England when the Shakers first were
organized but which gradually gave way to the uniform
white that became part of the mode of the classic revival. Beams, doors and window-sashes were painted blue
by the Shakers; the color, with its suggestion to them of
heaven—a cool heaven—is retained in Shaker buildings
to this day, though usually with some lightening of tone.
The Shaker scene, which also included the deep reds of
New England provincial furniture and tools, was by no
means lacking in color; its austerity came rather from the
effect of clarity, precision and extreme cleanliness. The
Shakers made a further ritual of cleaning, as symbolic of
the exorcise of sin.

Perhaps these closely interwoven unities were at the
heart of the antagonisms that repeatedly arose against
the Shakers. Because the sect so quickly attained a communal spirit which many were desiring during these rapidly changing, expansive years of the Republic, it may
have aroused a special unconscious envy. No doubt the
strangeness of the Shaker exercises, with the primitivism
which they desired or the paganism which they would
have abhorred, had its stirring effect. Anything suggestive
of secret rites aroused antagonism, particularly among
Puritan descendants in a stern New England and in upper
New York state, for many years, as was shown by the persistent movement against the Masons. But undoubtedly
it was the Shaker doctrines relating to sex that kept the

imagination of neighboring communities astir. The rough times of physical persecution endured by Mother Ann and her first followers were long since over; the attack now was less direct and mainly literary. A shower of pamphlets and books appeared about 1815, first directed against the Shakers because they had failed to bear arms in the War of 1812: their doctrines regarding non-resistance and peace were the target. Complications inevitably arose as to the disposal of property owned by those who entered the commune, in spite of what seemed an extreme effort toward honesty and fairness on the part of the Shakers. The major difficulties appeared when a husband or wife wished to become a Shaker and the other partner in marriage did not. The Shakers finally formulated a policy that excluded prospective members involved in such situations, but complexities arose, notably in the case of Mary Dyer and Eunice Chapman. These two set in motion a controversial literature, partly of their own writing, which spread over a space of some thirty years and casts an interesting light upon generally accepted formulas regarding the discussion of sex in this period. The case of Eunice Chapman was a replica in outline of that of Mary Dyer. Each claimed that her husband had taken from her both property and children, bestowing them upon the Shakers. Each fought to reclaim these, as well as the errant husband who had become a believer and made a great variety of charges against the Shakers in the process. But Mary Dyer's was the more complex instance, with a larger number of issues and publications and with more far-reaching sidelights in the matter of character and ways of living. Her first pamphlet was answered by one in rejoinder by her husband. Both husband and wife had the gift for portraying the concrete and special instance that is often the secret of the good novelist, and both used batteries of affidavits by neighbors and friends who likewise seemed to have an eye for concrete episodes and a flow of narrative. They indulged richly in portrayals of character of the Dyers and others who shared in their lives. Though the relation of the Dyers to the Shakers at New Lebanon made the final crux of these pamphlets, all the groundwork had a multiple story interest: the domestic habits, the ways of living of a whole community, the rise of errant personalities, as of certain traveling revivalists, became plain to the reader. In these accounts the forces of sex were discussed in vivid detail, even with psychological insight; the Dyers omitted very little that revealed their complex and changing marital relationship. In our histories of literature much has been made of the slow rise of the American novel, but here, in lively substance, as in outspoken debate, the very substance of the novel was exhibited with far more candor than in any English novel of the period or indeed of the entire nineteenth century. Only Fielding or Smollett could have matched it. When such tales of real life were publicly available the novel perhaps lacked a function. Joseph Dyer quit the race fairly early and his subsequent personal history is not altogether clear, but Mary Dyer continued to rewrite and elaborate her original work. A final edition was published in 1847 when she was an old woman, with the skilled assistance, one would guess, of an uncompromising enemy of the Shakers.

Mary Dyer's main charge was that "the Shaker spirit is magnetism, mingled with sexual passion," and in this she expressed the underlying contention of other critics. Some of these were detached observers of intelligence, and most of them had participated in Shaker life. The charges of immorality usually harked back to the initial period of Shaker history under Ann Lee. Of these, one of the earliest, *An Account of the People Called Shakers*, by Thomas Brown, published at Troy in 1812, was the most temperate. Brown had belonged to the society but was considered to have got hold of "the wrong chain." His book, which soon went into a second edition, was repudiated at first by the Shakers, but about seventy years later it was republished by them, with some softening revisions. The other more serious work of the same order, *A Countercheck to Shakerism*, by Samuel Brown, published in Cincinnati in 1824, was likewise a serious attempt to picture and analyze Shaker life with detachment, though with less fairness and sharper strictures. Both included testimonies from others. Both made an effort to achieve accuracy and even historical scholarship. Both attempted to explain Mother Ann's "sovereign address" and to attain a close view of her character as well as that of her followers. In this general literature, which contained many pamphleteering attacks upon the Shakers and some direct attacks upon them by those who had or said they had lived among them, there was an outstanding effect of realism, as in the works produced by the Dyers. It abounded in affidavits and "testimonies," often written with a sharp concreteness. Whatever the motives, and these were various, the case-histories were written to reveal or expose the life of the Shakers and the psychic phenomena peculiar to them. Limited though it was, this literature was not without general importance, and it showed what a long distance had been traversed since the period of colonial witchcraft when psychic and physical manifestations had produced fear, panic and a wave of destruction, with an insistence that these evidences were supernatural. Fear may have lain behind some of the attacks upon the Shakers. They themselves had no doubt that they were governed by supernatural powers in their strange dances, songs and early visions. But now a study of these phenomena had begun, the beginnings of psychological analysis. The method was empirical, even behavioristic. The studies were indeed case-histories, though not so called.

As for the circumstances described in these writings, their factual basis must have been difficult to establish. Ann and William Lee had died nearly thirty years before any one of them was undertaken, and the writers drew upon the memories of old men and women on subjects

that have always lent themselves to distortion. Some of
the gross accounts may seem to have a semblance of
truth, since the rejection of what the Shakers called "carnal nature" was so vehement as to indicate an intense preoccupation with it. The believers may have verged upon
experiences which they consciously abhorred; yet, whatever were the hidden sources of Mother Ann's power, two
circumstances cannot easily be explained in these terms.
She attracted to the Shaker belief men and women of high
character, standing and unusual intelligence, and she herself both embodied and taught precepts of thrift, neatness
and industry that are not consonant with rude orgies.
These precepts became rules of life in the Shaker communities. No saying was more frequently on the lips of
Shakers than "By their fruits ye shall know them," and
the fruits were almost continuously visible from the first
published utterance of the Shakers in 1790, simple, re-
strained and within its narrow limits full of plain dignity.
The early "testimonies" relating to Shaker life, existing in
a wealth of manuscripts, have the same quality. One of
the sharpest of the pamphleteers, writing in 1822, ad-
mitted that he could not "fault" the three leading Shakers
whom he had known well in trade for their sanctity, honesty and integrity. Shaker fairness in matters of trade
quickly became a by-word throughout New England, and
even their enemies acknowledged, in numerous affidavits,
that the Shakers excelled in the mechanical arts.

The low valley at New Lebanon with its narrow irregu-

lar rising tiers had become the site of the first organized
Shaker community. The region had a severe and quiet
beauty, but the soil had deteriorated because of over-
cultivation before the Shakers bought it. Agriculture on
a broad scale was therefore impossible, and the Shakers
set up trades, harness-making, weaving, chair-making.
The industrial unit was the "family," which might embrace
a number of natural families. From the first, the chair-
making was notable. At Watervliet, chairs were said to
have been made for sale as early as 1776, and the Shakers
later claimed to have been the first to engage in the business. Certainly they were among the first to initiate what
may be called mass-production, although it was their
craftsmanship that was to make them famous. Part of this
was no doubt derived from honest traditions in furniture-
making that were long since established in New England,
but the Shaker way of life heightened certain of their
inherent qualities. The Shakers loved symmetry, and balances were fundamental in their faith. Work had a special
sanction from Mother Ann in the oft-repeated, "Put your
hands to work, your hearts to God," which was echoed
even in a song of praise. Perhaps the influence of Dutch
provincial craftsmanship encountered at Watervliet by
the early Shakers and by others who frequently traveled
there in later years had some effect in heightening the
simple severity belonging to Shaker crafts, yet this quality was also evident in the home-made provincial furniture of New England. What the Shakers added was a re-

finement of the inevitable principle of economy, a more exquisite sense of symmetry, which they truly loved and which expressed to them the "eternal two." Economy was a necessity in their first years; it soon became an esthetic principle, lovingly applied, with the result that their plain forms approached but never quite overstepped the border of the sensuous. The governing principle was that which appeared early in their hymns of praise. These objects were made for temporal use and should not exceed clear and simple requirements. The fact that such uses were transitory in the Shaker view, because of their acceptance of cycles of change, meant no slackening of applied skills. The Millennium had come; these objects were made under the arch of eternity, and some of them, with their perfection of workmanship, still seemed destined to last for an extended portion of it.

Oval boxes with lids of varying sizes for many uses were made early by the Shakers, who also developed broom-making, still a new industry, creating brooms for a large variety of uses with great ingenuity and efficiency, even with passion; the Shaker love of cleanliness, appearing in one of their characteristic ceremonials, seemed to give their skill in this direction a special impetus. In their tailoring shop, first set up to make clothes for believers, simple clothing was also made for worldly customers. With their own looms, carding machines and fulling mills, they made cloth. In 1814 a flood running through the New Lebanon valley destroyed these machines and the mill, several hundred yards of cloth and the chair-makers' shop, with a large number of finished chairs. The loss ran to almost $12,000. The quick recovery of the community from this catastrophe indicated both the Shaker skill in organization and the substantial reputation they had achieved in industry. The next year they built a trip-hammer dam beside the new chair factory in order to utilize water-power on a larger scale, and sent a donation of three hundred dollars to the inhabitants of Petersburg, Virginia, who had suffered a severe loss by fire. Such gifts by the Shakers—a testimony to their thrift as well as to their generosity—were not uncommon and indicated as well the social equability which they had achieved, per-mitting them to offer amenities to "the world." A few years later they sent five hundred dollars to the city of Troy, which had also been badly damaged by fire.

The early pressure of need with the inclusion among the first believers of men or women with a turn for inven-tion may account in part for the extraordinary outflower-ing of invention and the use of mechanical devices among the Shakers. As early as 1790, one of the brothers invented and made a machine for setting card-teeth. Somewhat later, as the tailoring shops grew with the expansion of the communities and with outside trade, a machine was invented for the cutting of cloth in quantity. A screw-propeller—the invention of Thomas Wells at Watervliet—was made and used by him before this device had come into general use, one of the many parallel inventions of this order springing up at the end of the eighteenth century. A turbine water-wheel is said to have been invented at New Lebanon, and a home-made threshing machine was made there in 1815. The right to use mechanical devices was frequently bought from their inventors by the Shakers; in some instances it is difficult to distinguish precisely between these and others which the Shakers themselves invented or perfected. But there can be no doubt as to their constant preoccupation with the processes of mechanical invention or the prolific use which they made of them. They possessed the Yankee inheritance. By far the greater number of their members in the East and many in the West came from New England or that portion of upper New York which was substantially New England, yet this circumstance fails to account entirely for the marked Shaker bent in this direction. Undoubtedly the use of mechanics and the incidence of invention was far higher among the Shakers than in similar communities of the same size in the outside world. Given the impetus of need and of Yankee ingenuity, the reasons may be found in other factors. It was not only in the crafts and in mechanics that the Shakers exhibited a notable skill. By 1794 they were advertising the sale of garden seeds at New Lebanon. Almost immediately botanical gardens were established there, with the cultivation of medicinal herbs. The minute and even exquisite care required for these products perhaps would have suited the Shakers better than large-scale farming, even if the condition of

the soil at New Lebanon had made this possible. The
Shakers had a genius for choosing beautiful sites for their
communities; each one included fine contours of land
with either lakes or streams, but the soil tended to be
rocky and in many cases was exhausted: this was no
doubt the immediate reason why most of them followed
New Lebanon in producing seeds. Shakers with seed-
wagons began traveling through eastern and central New
York as early as 1812. The annual production of seeds at
New Lebanon soon reached two thousand pounds a year
and often exceeded that amount. Shaker seed-wagons
moved in the spring in all directions from all the communities, with some brisk conflicts as to territories belonging
to each one. These were easily resolved; a larger temptation lay in the possibility of mixing seeds "of the world"
with their own. But whatever the possible enlargement
of profits, it was decided that this practice would bring
"loss upon the joint interest and dishonor upon the gospel." Therefore an agreement was signed not to sell "any
seeds to the world which are not raised among believers
(excepting melon seeds)." The reason for this exception
is not clear. Perhaps when a sufficient number of New
England pumpkins had been grown on the few small
tracts of level land, not enough space remained for
melons. Perhaps to the Shakers with their passion for
order and symmetry these sprawling vines were not
pleasing.

Whatever the Shakers turned their hands to seemed to

be accomplished not only well but with a final perfection of workmanship. Their seeds were put up in simple but exquisitely designed and printed packages. Their aptitude for the handicrafts appeared in many details, in finely woven braids for upholstery and beautifully finished woodwork for their buildings. Their beginnings had been poor, with the first houses of roughly hewn logs; they had lacked food. As one brother plaintively remarked, they had "scarcely any pie." What they achieved within a remarkably short time was not only prosperity or even a sufficient abundance. It was something that may be described as creative fluency. Their favorite balances were achieved: agriculture was offset by mechanics, the finer handicrafts by blacksmithing, the making of hoes and small tools—the Shakers were among the first to manufacture cut nails—as well as the making of bricks and shingles. All were willing to undertake common tasks, and a measure of rotation seemed to make possible the full use of Shaker gifts.

No doubt the practical, organizing powers of Lucy Wright and the elders and eldresses who worked with her had much to do with the establishment of a good economy within which this variety of activities could flourish. No doubt too the fact that the Shakers were closely homogeneous in race, social experience and religious tradition made for ease in communal undertakings. Their beliefs meant a radical departure from tradition, but dissent itself was traditional in New England

and conflict between sects had been manifest there since
the first appearance of the Quakers in Boston. In the
stress upon the Puritan tradition, it is sometimes forgotten
that the people of New England were inured to dissent,
that Puritanism itself was dissent. All these factors tended
to create the firmly wrought social groundwork that creative forces seem to require. "Union" was of course ardently sought by the Shakers, but their related experiences, what they called "travel" and "labor," both of
which were in some sense intellectual and concentrated,
made a lively underply for all their activities. That there
was nothing static in their beliefs must account in some
measure for their productivity. Notably what they created
was all of a piece; it was all social, all functional, all for
use, chairs, tables, labor-saving devices, seeds, herbs.
Perhaps their philosophy of change gave the Shakers still
further creative strength, permitting flexible adaptations
and a free flow of inherent creative powers.

That the Shakers never practiced the decorative arts,
never ventured into any known use of pencil or brush,
may be explained on grounds other than their convictions.
They were English by descent, almost invariably; an occasional name suggests an alteration from French origins,
but hardly another exception appears. Like other New
Englanders they lacked a tradition in the decorative arts,
not, as has been frequently said, because of Puritan sup-
pressions but because the English had never created the
decorative folk-arts, as had the peoples of continental

Europe, even before the advent of Puritanism. The abstract strain which had run through all New England thought was dominant among the Shakers; their repudiation of ornament sprang from their rejection of the world and its vanities, but this in turn was consonant with a lack of familiarity with the language of ornament. A few watercolor or wash or pencil drawings of Shaker villages were made at an early period of an order which may be designated as folk-art, mathematical, delicate, unsophisticated, but these, whether made secretly by Shakers or by others who were self-taught, only prove the absence of a decorative tradition, just as their abstract handling suggests a prevailing mode of thought, however homely or untutored. The repeated Shaker use of the word "type" or "typical," as in "typical dancing," is an index to their prevailing habits of mind. "Typical dancing" was dancing which revealed the essential spirit, an archetypal holiness, and which brought this to believers. Yet the abstract was by no means the vague; the strain was powerful. It appeared unmistakably in their crafts and in their architecture. Here the mode was carried into clear designs. Natural forms are never even vaguely suggested. Pure line, exquisite balances, severe masses, finely finished surfaces make the whole esthetic vocabulary of their work.

Within the space of a generation the Shakers, comparatively small in numbers but widely distributed as to their communities and their influence, had become a folk. They possessed the coherence and unity of a folk, the instinctive traditional habits and beliefs, and the arts that have belonged to folk-groups. They exhibited those primitive elements which have always belonged to the folk-imagination and use the typical forms of folk-expression, dance and song, the crafts, communal customs, even communal language.

A Note on Folklore

PLENTY of scorn is abroad as to the folk, the folksy, folk-song, folklore—and quite rightly too. We have probably heard enough of "Barb'ry Allen" and the minute variations displayed in that lovely ballad as sung in remote corners of these States. Folk-songs have been set like rosettes on the surface of plays and novels, and quaint old American furniture has been so precisely and ardently described in the course of a narrative that one can fairly see the antique-dealer at the door. In a recent short story a quilt is thrown over a dead woman at a climactic moment, and the pattern of the quilt—a rare pattern—is mentioned; of course the sense of human fate is destroyed on the instant. If the quilt were the only piece of antiquarianism the story as a whole might have survived, as stories do sometimes seem to survive maltreatment; but it is a mosaic of folk-oddments, and the situation never works itself through.

This placing of quaint bits end to end has appeared among us since the seventies, and it has often indicated an acute sense of classes. This was shown in the work of one who has had insufficient recognition as a forerunner in folk or regional literature, Mrs. Stowe, whose early

sketches and later novels for better or worse were opening
salvos of the local color movement. In her day there was
still an immense failure to assimilate the democratic idea,
even among plain people like the Beechers. The use of
the word "lady" as a title until a late period was a sign;
and the sense of classes was continually being reinforced
by the influx of those quaint and useful creatures, the immigrants, as well as by the sub-stratification of the Negro.
Mrs. Stowe always regarded the lower orders as lower
orders, and when she could not view them with humor
she provided a lavish pity—another revelation of the su-
perior attitude. The effort to create social distances has
appeared steadily ever since in the universal American
desire to rise higher than the folk—to become, as Ruth
Suckow has said, "folks." When a sufficient degree of social eminence has been achieved it has often been possible
to consider the folk delightful, and to remember and read
about them with a mild nostalgia.

Some of the nostalgia is undoubtedly genuine. In the
process of changing from folk to folks many things have
been lost, a sense of the arts, for example, and instinctive
taste. Those who climb laboriously and artificially usually
lose the play of instinct, and so may feel a wistful enthusiasm for quilts, wood-carvings, songs, rich language and
other creative fragments that are natural folk-possessions.
Then too the folk show a coherence lacking in our unstable and heterogeneous social life. It is this that makes
the underply of the best of the folk-novels and even ap-

pears in many of the poorer ones, with the result that it is possible to gain from them what the American novel too often has failed to offer, translation into a consistent world. And almost every touch of these folk-possessions—language, carvings, and so on—reveals those ties with the natural world which are now being acutely missed in a machine civilization. More than one critic has suggested that recent folk-novels have been received with eagerness because they offer temporary release from the consciousness of overgrown cities and the machine.

To all this the reply of the social critic is prompt and thoroughly valid: "regression" sums it up. The life thus portrayed is a survival of the past, and these novels have usually failed to recognize that basic circumstance, with a resulting incompleteness, as when any large element in a human situation is disregarded. At their best they have seldom developed major themes. The most sympathetic criticism is obliged to admit that they do not often belong within the larger areas of literature. Pedantry, a mild snobbishness, a mild sentimental glow are at one end of the scale; at the other, affection and genuine absorption. For the large ends of literature even affection and absorption are not enough. Social critics and literary critics may unite in setting down this movement as confused and apparently wandering. But, doing so, they cannot dispose of it. The movement toward an appropriation of our folk-life and folk-expression has gone on in spite of criticism or neglect. It antedates many current literary movements and may outlast some of them. It is as old as the life of the nation. A lively sense of our localized native speech, folk-ways, folk-humor, developed soon after the Revolution. By the thirties and forties these had found a wide place in popular stories and on the stage, and a sub-literary handling of folk-heroes and folk-tales continued throughout the century. Even the literary approach to these materials is not new, and a few early efforts were made toward scholarship and criticism. Some of these were not very substantial; much of the literary handling bears a date stamped upon it. But the movement has been sustained; and a singular circumstance lies in the fact that it has been carried on by any number of widely separated individuals who have found these materials attractive and have made discoveries of their own.

Here and there little swirls of connection are discernible among their efforts, as in that body of southwestern comic lore that began to find its way into print in the eighteen thirties, forties and fifties. But even in this no concerted purpose appeared; it has been in the main an underground movement. Almost anyone who has been searching for materials in a given locality has come across cabinet-makers, paper-hangers, master-plumbers, doctors, lawyers, in considerable numbers, whose secret life-work seems to have been the collection and mulling over of native songs, dance-tunes, stories, old remembrances and folk-talk; and their interest seems a spontaneous growth. Even now, when this movement has begun to attract criti-

cal attention, many single books with a bias toward these
materials are being produced by individuals who are not
writers or students in an ordinary sense at all but who,
working more or less alone, seem to be driven by a warm
sense of possession to communicate what they have discovered. This sense of possession has had in itself something of the breadth and unstudied character of a folk-
movement; and its invasions are wider than is commonly
recognized. When the literary uses of these materials have
been considered the folk-novel or folk-play has usually become the focus of discussion: but folk-materials have appeared with an almost consistent emphasis in recent
poetry from Vachel Lindsay to Hart Crane; a whole
school of biography has developed whose work perhaps
is not biography at all but an accumulation of legends
that have gathered around certain striking native figures,
particularly of the West. Folklore and folk-ways have
made a true groundwork for autobiography, as in Way-
man Hogue's sensitive, pliant *Back Yonder*, and a considerable amount of lone pioneering has been done by
writers who have struck boldly into untouched folk-materials, formulating interpretations of great social and
historical importance.

Lloyd Lewis's *Myths After Lincoln* is such a piece of
pioneering. That Lincoln is a folk-hero has long been
known, but only in a general sense. Mr. Lewis has succeeded in giving strange and substantial outline to the
generalization, and his book shows the primitive myth-

making faculty at work among us, not in some isolated
pocket of the Cumberlands or the Ozarks, but on a broad
scale throughout the country, at a late date. This impressive study creates a new understanding of the American
character of the period, and might serve as a foundation
for an estimate of certain essential movements of the
American mind. George Pullen Jackson's *White Spirituals
of the Southern Uplands* also has a value far beyond its
notable contribution to the technical study of folk-song.
Tracing the course of these spirituals, Dr. Jackson has
discovered and revealed widespread groups still existing
in the South and Southwest who behave like "folks" but
who have kept certain qualities of folk-life and folk-expression; and this broad study could also be freely used
by historians, sociologists and other students of the mass
mind if they would match Dr. Jackson's ardor and com-
petence with their own.

Naturally confusion and incompletion are apparent in
all this. No other people has created its folklore and tried
to assimilate it and turn it to the purposes of the creative
imagination and of self-understanding, all within a brief
span. Among other peoples the appropriation of such materials has been immensely slow; literary uses have followed gradually, often at a distance of centuries. The
wonder is that a people whose elements have been far
from homogeneous should have steadily created a distinctive lore from its earliest days, and that the hold among
us upon these materials should have been so stubborn

against all the forces of a modern civilization which tend to scatter them to the four winds. It is as if a widespread instinct were at work to create and learn them by heart before it is too late; and, if the history of other peoples is a sign, this instinct has been sound. In such materials lies a large common storage of experience and character. Probably we are still a folk—an imperfectly formed folk— rather than a schooled and civilized people. This fate is strange enough in a modern world, but from the beginning we have also had another destiny. We are also acutely conscious and self-conscious, critical and purposive. Our literature and public speech are strewn with the evidences of this from the days of the founding fathers onward. Conflicting forces have thus been set up, but we shall hardly be able to select another course at this late date, and it would seem possible at times to use one strain on behalf of the other.

Instead of insisting on the impossible, critics might accomplish more by a skilled and knowledgeable evaluation of the many more or less humble works at hand. To say, as has been said, that a given folk-novel is not heroic or that it fails to illuminate human life on a large scale is to apply, very flatteringly, standards which are seldom applied to other fiction. The heroic cannot be expected to spring up like a jack-in-the-box, and illumination of human life on a large scale has never been an everyday event in literary history. These folk-novels often achieve only the simplest of the intentions of the novel: to pre-

sent a phase of life that is new, new to most of us. They
often do this well; and other uses of these materials in
the play or the biography frequently accomplish much
the same thing. They are informative mainly. As for the
larger offices of criticism, there are plenty of chances for
these also here. A whole area lies nearly vacant, to be revealed and possessed by criticism, that of form. The
changes in form going on at present are apparently profound, and they seem to bear a close relation to changes
in the social fabric. It would perhaps be too much to say
that these alterations are related in origin to the emergence of folklore, but the free use of the informal tale (as
opposed to the short story), the sketch, the chronicle, the
poetic structures, for the transliteration of folk-materials,
has certainly provided momentum. Even in the folk-
drama and the narrative, where failures may so easily be
pointed out, subtle advances have been made. This is apparent in Roark Bradford's *John Henry*, a little epic, half
fantasy, stripped to the core of tragedy. The type has appeared in many brief plays and most notably in *The
Green Pastures*, which united the outlines of the chronicle
play with those of choral drama. In the annual *Folk-Say*,
which Mr. B. A. Botkin has assembled almost single-
handed for a number of years, not only is a great variety
of traditional materials uncovered but the handling almost consistently shows a break with set patterns.

The freer and simpler, more primitive and often poetic
forms, such as the rhapsody, the monologue, the tale, de-

veloped early among us. They were particularly marked in approaches to folk-materials. Their rise was apparently spontaneous and natural, whereas late and civilized forms like the novel seem to have been imposed. The stringent exactions of the full-length, highly organized novel have often lain heavily upon our hesitating, experimental writing. In many instances the primitive forms have slid away into the sketch, the chronicle, and other semi-literary modes of expression; and the opportunities are still abundant for their full and natural furtherance, for their genuine outflowering. To reveal the rise and pressure of forms in our literature—in our whole literature, including folk-literature—to show where fulfillment has been impeded and by what forces would mean the articulation of large traditions which now are regarded as minor or are vaguely known as subterranean. Writers hesitate with a sense of uncertain experiment when they might move with freedom if the integrity of the traditions that lie behind them were made clear.

A lasting confusion as to the uses of folk-language suggests what clarity of critical purpose might accomplish. Almost periodically dialect is rendered with awkward force. On another tack the "fine-pretty" qualities of folk-language are handled with considerable license. What is wanted of course is not the grotesquerie or the decorations but the essence of speech. The differences involved are between language as a means of record and language as a medium of expression, and this distinction in turn

relates itself to certain often-repeated esthetic first principles. In the matter of speech the mere record has value,
even when this appears in unlikely and unattractive aspects, since much of our popular speech may be discovered only in fragments and many of the fragments are in
danger of being lost. These are needed to establish and
confirm our often faltering sense of the American language. At the same time a genuine esthetic criticism of
the native language as a medium is also needed; and this
would necessarily rest upon a grounding in native speech
which no great number of critics seem to have. Our own
traditions in the matter of folk-language are not brought
into useful play. A hundred years ago, Seba Smith created
an effect of Yankee speech without making its oddities
obtrusive, in a medium that is all but transparent, and, if
one cares to notice it, very beautiful, revealing without
effort the slow abundant satire. A small number of now
forgotten writers accomplished something of the same
effect at about the same time; indeed within that formative period many of the characteristic rhythms and colors
of American speech became clear. But these early conquests were nearly obliterated by Lowell's attempt at a
crackling realism in *The Biglow Papers*, and many another
dark abyss in the use of the native language yawned afterward. Occasionally the more sensitive uses have been
maintained; but in the intervening years these have generally been forgotten, and it is probably safe to say that
many writers of the present day who use folk materials,

even within the New England tradition, do not know the work of the quiet journalist of Maine. In college courses *The Biglow Papers* are likely to have a place when Seba Smith's *Downing Papers*—in all ways true originals, and of far greater social importance—are neglected. Such neglect may come in part from our wistful bias toward an aristocratic literature. Some of it comes from a situation which has perhaps been inevitable in a country where folk-processes have been strong. Your folk is never conscious of literary values or implications. Such materials have slipped from view with others of folk-origin, and many of them are buried or all but lost.

All this opens possibilities for criticism and scholarship of a most radical, refreshing kind. Probably few individuals are equipped to teach courses in American folklore, equipped in the usual scholastic sense. The subject is still barely recognized. In a recent survey of the teaching of American literature by Alice Louise LeFevre, eighty colleges and universities were considered, of wide geographical distribution, of varying size, origin and alliances. By design, a number of institutions were included where an interest in folk-materials on the part of one or more teachers was known to exist. No one of the eighty offers a course in American folklore. At Duke University, an admirable regional approach has been made; the folklore of North Carolina is presented against a background of ancient balladry and the primitive lore of other countries, and students are encouraged to collect and consider the lore of their native sections. At the University of Oklahoma, American folklore is included in a general course, and lectures are offered that tend to build up that consciousness of the natural scene which interpenetrates folkexpression and seems essential for a full life in any region. They touch upon natural history and geology in Oklahoma, while others deal with the southwestern desert, the history of Mexico and life in the old South. Undergraduate courses are given on the Indians of Oklahoma—a peculiarly fruitful subject, since Indian history in this state reveals a little known cross-section of American life. The regional idea of saturation in the whole life of the geographic section has thus invaded a natural sphere, that of education. But recognition of American folklore as an entire subject still lags behind.

Accordingly, one of those rare and perfect situations exists in which the teachers would know little more than the students and could invade uncharted areas with them. The subject now seems to await the kind of thoroughgoing treatment that colleges and universities could well give, with their many resources, with the steady possibility of showing new perspectives through work which they have already established. The subvention of funds, fellowships, foundations will be needed, for the many buried materials lie deep and the slag surrounding fine pieces of expression is often plentiful. Even with such assistance the approaches cannot be easy. An immense amount of exploration and synthesis is to be accomplished. Whole strains of expression are still to be brought together and their continuities made clear. But whatever the demands or difficulties, these pursuits would remain highly exciting, even adventurous. Probably nothing can equal the impetus created by a long free oral tradition, and this we lack, except in a few localities. But *liaisons* with the past could be formed which might in part make up for the absence; and none of this would be "regression," for the view would or should be unsentimental, and the materials would consist at bottom of generic elements which still in some fashion endure.

The heroic may not appear in consequence. Literary appropriation might not be hastened; this might even be delayed and perhaps should be, to offset a precocious growth. The process would be that of settling in. The imaginative folk-life of our short past could gradually become a free possession, with the chance that its persistent patterns of thought and feeling and form would eventually flow into natural use. The many coherences of folk-life might be seen to possess lasting social values. If the social critic, the literary critic and the student-scholar really joined in these undertakings, something like a full perception of our culture or cultures might follow.

Voltaire Combe

THE QUEER NAME is not an invention. It belongs
to an obscure artist born in Jordan on the Erie Canal,
who may have been called Voltaire by way of comic dis-
illusionment. A great depression was under way. The
year of his birth was 1837.

Jordan had grown into a tough prosperity because of
the canal: the doorways of its groceries and groggeries,
taverns and bawdy houses opened upon slow waters that
were often crowded with boats waiting to pass through
the locks a mile to the west. A few grist mills and wood-
working factories had been established; and lush springs
pouring from a green hillside helped produce a whiskey
that could be had for a nickel a glass, or, if a jug was
carried up the hill, for ten cents a gallon. By no means in
the genteel tradition, Jordan survived the depression and
for many years presented a strong phase of the American
scene. The canal was something of a frontier; the canawlers were warmly colored variants of the boatmen who had
long commanded our waterways. Neighboring farmers
come from strong Yankee stock; they looked it, spoke it.
Newly arrived Irishmen, of the legion scattering over the
country, made barrels and added their surplus of con-

vivial256y and song. Small circuses and troupes of players, who early found an audience among us, often tarried in Jordan, while even the more respectable inhabitants had their typical qualities: they tolerated ripe transgressions since these lowered taxes.

Never was a place less likely to produce art, if popular theories may be accepted. On our frontiers and indeed elsewhere throughout the long period of our early development we are supposed to have been too much occupied by the utilitarian business of living to concern ourselves with art, too much on the move to permit that residue of social experience to form from which the artist in one way or another must draw. If art appeared, the genteel tradition is said to have paralyzed it. A candid view of the rougher aspects of American life is supposed not to have emerged in painting until the "Eight" or the so-called "ashcan school" began to picture them about 1912. The American scene has been considered the discovery of the present generation.

The career of Voltaire Combe, unobtrusive though it was, upsets some of these conclusions. He began to draw as a small boy, but he was by no means regarded as an oddity. Limners freely plied their trade in and about Jordan during these years, painting portraits and occasional landscapes for fifteen or twenty dollars apiece. The young Voltaire may have known a nearby provincial sculptor who carved portraits in basswood and colored them to the life, sometimes portraying all the children of a family life size, with a formal realism. A tall poly-chromed peacock, finely stylized, came out of this region, which was certainly not made for use, not even for a cir-cus merry-go-round, but was obviously carved for pleas-ure.

It was the limners who set Voltaire on his way; he knew them, always honored them, and from them per-haps gained the idea that the artist was mainly the artisan, the honest journeyman. In later years he insisted that anyone could learn to paint. But somewhere he gained another view, perhaps when as a boy of fourteen he went on foot to Syracuse and pulled the doorbell of a minor painter living there, "an ideal artist in appearance," who wore a velvet coat and had a studio with all the appur-tenances. Before long he began to consider the artist as a singular being; at least he tended to regard himself in that light. He was small, with what one of the villagers called "a pouter-pigeon look." Like many of our earlier small-town characters he was something of an actor. He developed a pose and a vocabulary that were a long way from Jordan. As a boy he had seen Fanny Elssler; he would apostrophize her dancing in silky sentences. Prowl-ing around he managed to discover a good deal of Ameri-can art and would discourse on "realms of poet artists breathing classic song" and on Cole's "Zenobian accents."

But it was one of the engaging aspects of Combe's character that he could take on a good deal of overlay without much alteration of a fundamental core. Still off on the romantic strain, he enlisted when the Civil War broke out, but in the cavalry, not the infantry, buying himself a mettlesome horse and a finely chased sword with a gold and ivory handle, and obviously expecting an officer's rank. He was made a bugler. At least he returned after three years with sketchbooks filled with pictures of himself in the thick of dramatic events. One of these, which he afterward developed in oil, showed him reading *Faust* by candlelight in an army tent, and was entitled "Before Ball's Bluff."

After Combe moved to New York, about 1870, he seems to have painted pictures occasionally for the growing swarm of lithographers; probably he did hand coloring for some of them, and he may have sold a picture now and again to others, yet how he made a living at any time remains something of a mystery. He managed to travel a good deal, wandering down into Maryland and Virginia. His increasingly courtly, persuasive manner was perhaps no handicap to him in finding the means to get about, or to stay where he wished to stay. By 1880 he was returning to Jordan for long summers.

Its roystering era had begun to dwindle even before the Civil War, when a new railroad brought in manufactured goods that drove the small local factories out of business and carried away most of the grain crops. Traffic on the canal grew sluggish. Derelicts from a better time now sat in grocery doorways or on barrels outside—"waiting," Combe said, "always waiting." Old canawlers were

there, stranded farmers, an old circus performer, a danc-
ing-master, left high but not dry—not while Voltaire
could buy them a tumbler of whiskey, which could still
be had in back rooms for a nickel. When he first went
back, "some adopted a mode of non-recognition," he
said, "due to jealousy." He wore a Prince Albert and a
derby; one of the citizens remarked that "when he walked
down one side of the street the other side tipped." But
he knew how to thaw them out: this was where his heart
lay. They soon were calling him Captain Combe, then
Cap; they went fishing with him at Cross Lake, camped,
and saluted the dawn. Some of them fiddled or played
the guitar. So did Voltaire. Others might slip into a jog
or a clog. Cap Combe could foot it lightly, and they
would all bawl out "Old Dan Tucker" or "Zip Coon,"
"Rosin the Bow" or "Lord Ullin's Daughter," or other
old songs with many stanzas to which they could add
lyrical lines of their own.

These people were what Combe called "distinct." Eas-
ing them into characteristic attitudes he sketched them
again and again, later working up the sketches into full
paintings. By the end of the eighties or early nineties he
had portrayed most of these old wastrels, without con-
descension or sentimentality. In "Old Dan Tucker and
His Recreant Son" a youth with a handsome, mobile countenance is seated on a rickety, shuck-bottomed chair with
a fiddle under his arm, a hand on a bottle; this figure,
who appears in a number of the pictures, may have repre-

sented Combe himself as a lad or perhaps was one of his
younger friends. The youth is looking toward an old man
in a shabby bright-blue coat, tall white hat, whitey-gray
trousers—the Yankee costume of an earlier generation—
who with a look of race and a shattered air is giving
stubborn attention to one of the lighter pleasures.

In "The Old Dancing Master Shows How Fanny Elssler
Danced a Pas Deux" the scene is a loft, the color key low,
the handling of darks and guttering lights bold yet un-
theatrical. A lad is fiddling; a sprawling figure, pictured
without reserve, is wholly sunk. The tall old dancing-
master in a battered high hat, worn ballet shoes, with fly-
ing coattails, his fiddle and bow still in one hand, is
tripping it lightly with a look of great absorption. One
knows that his life was dedicated to the arts, to nice dis-
tinctions, and to failure. The fourth figure, a Yankee
farmer who was cast early in life for a deacon, stout, red-
faced, with a fringe of white beard, his mouth set in
a grim line, has let his fiddle drop to his knees and has
turned to see the show: he finds it almost too wild a
spectacle.

A severe critic might say that Combe failed to understand the medium of water color, gouache, or tempera
which he almost consistently employed for these pictures
and for the few portraits that belong with this group.
He used a light medium like oil, with an effect of under-
painting, with great care to build up solid bodies, a
minute circumspection as to detail. He had a special

aptitude for depicting old hands, old faces, the thin
crinkled skin with an underlying flush, a weathered look.
He dwelt upon the textures of frayed coats, worn boots,
a bandanna, the polished wood of a fiddle: it was as if
no lavish effort could be too much. The effect is sometimes labored, occasionally a little woolly; we may admit
that there is something rustic about these paintings. But
at least in "The Old Dancing Master" and perhaps in
others Combe contrived a liberal arrangement out of
difficult elements with great skill, and he consistently
achieved what he set out to achieve: the portrayal of
character. These people carry the irreducible element in
their faces, their figures. They concentrate histories, with
a sharp edge.

Later, when he no longer went back to Jordan, Combe
began what he called a novel, whose characters were Dan
Tucker and the rest, whose structure was of the simplest
order: to create the effect of motion he simply moved
his people away from Jordan and around the country
where they foregathered in places he had particularly
enjoyed, encountered people he had admired, some of
them historical figures, among them Henry Clay and
John Randolph of Roanoke. The time was hazy; the de-
scriptions of the American countryside were long, loving,
full. Paragraphs were devoted to the transparent brilliance of sassafras leaves in autumn, to the white rush
of waters down sandy gulleys in the South, to a richly
fruited summer. All the characters were seen under a

golden ray. Scarcely a touch appears of the salty actu-
ality which distinguishes the Jordan paintings. The style
was idyllic, even touched at times by the airy elegance
which Combe had picked up somewhere along the way;
but the sentiment was genuine. He worked on the long
allegory for years, writing and rewriting it, piling up a
great stack of manuscript.

An inveterate collector, he managed to get together
copies of the old readers, romances, song-books, geog-
raphies, and even magazines like *Brother Jonathan* which
he had known as a boy. He also collected Surtees, Smollett, Dickens; many of his paintings of this later time were
derived from literary sources. He pictured Bardolph,
Pistol, and Dame Quickly as he conceived them; for
years, he said, he sought for a Bardolphian nose, to create one from nature, and found it at last on a Jersey ferry,
only to fail of his object because Bardolph's wife was
wounded by the idea. Some of these pictures were highly
florid: Undine floating downstream in blue tulle, or a
diabolic vermilion-clad Mephistopheles peering over the
shoulder of a buxom Marguerite.

None of them was strictly genteel, none of them sold,
least of all those of the Jordan group. With impressionism to the fore, their painstaking method was as much
against them as their subjects. Combe was confused and
tormented by impressionism, bitter about the ascendancy
of French art. He spoke darkly of a painting refused by
the Academy because it would have killed everything

within fifty feet of it. Toward the end, by a curious fate, he found himself in a Middlewestern town, with an occasional photograph to enlarge in crayon or copy in oil; but he read of the Armory show and wrote a long article on art which he felt was "needed." Through it ran a kind of hoarse pathos. "Is art retrograding in America? Yes, when compared with the art of seventy years ago, for then the nearest approach to nature was the artist's aim. What is art? Is it the capacity to depict undefined departures of eccentric pencils and technical exaggerations? The latest in art is not the highest. Pupils, learn to draw at home—not in Paris! Patronize American art, ye moneyed Americans!"

At the end the effect of pose was gone. Combe wore the hurt, exposed look that sometimes comes over the faces of old people; yet he seems to have entertained no overwhelming sense of grievance because his work was not accepted or understood. He died in 1916. Common folk who saw the Jordan pictures in these last years regarded them as suitable for barrooms; those with greater sophistication were sure that story-telling in art had gone forever. But Combe was not a story-teller, except as character may comprise a story. He may be related to the genre painters from Mount to Eastman Johnson, whose work he knew well, but he exceeded most of them in gusto. Their people tend to become figures in a picturesque scene. With Combe character is foreground in all senses. His ancestry lies rather among the limners

whom he knew as a boy, though he abandoned their
primitivism. He may even be linked with some of our
more acknowledged early portrait painters, whose sense
of character was often transcendent, though they seldom
if ever chose subjects, as Combe did, from homely and
unprosperous levels.

His Jordan group, as it happens, was painted some
ten years or more before "McSorley's Bar," which has
been considered as inaugurating an era of candor. "Mc-
Sorley's Bar" is a far finer accomplishment than anything
Combe produced, and Sloan—a member of the "Eight"
—was able to put his conviction as to free subjects in
motion. Combe seems to have had no influence at all;
most of his works are now scattered or have disappeared.
Yet the pattern of his life dispels certain ideas as to the
pervasiveness of the genteel tradition. His career suggests that the impulse toward art may have had a wider
spread in our nascent civilization than we have surmised.
We have often pictured ourselves with eyes on the hori-
zon, magnetized by the future, seldom looking backward:
yet here and there we have had a wish for commemoration. Combe had it; fragmentary evidence of the same
compulsion is coming to light from many out-of-the-way
corners in paintings, often by untutored individuals who
set down what they saw and felt about scenes or people
whom they knew well. Perhaps the history of American
art or its major directions cannot be understood until
these minor, even personal works are taken into account.

They have arisen in all periods, and they may have something to say as to the American character.

In a formal history of American art Voltaire Combe might achieve only a mention or a footnote, if as much. In a broadly compassed social study he and others like him would have an essential place; and surely he deserves a niche for the odd way in which his own character was compounded. Combe really admired gentility. He chose his subjects, it would seem, almost in spite of himself. For one who was convival it could not have been altogether easy to work without the urgency of others headed in the same direction.

Traditions for a Negro Literature

THE ONSET of plays and novels about the Negro in the last eight or ten years, the vogue of the spirituals, the rise of jazz, and the slender outcroppings of a literature by Negro writers has produced a familiar American response—a cult. Even the usual note of salvation has not been lacking: these primitive elements, it has been urged, will invigorate a slack native art. The ecstasies of the cult have been followed by the inevitable reaction. Productions which have the Negro as a subject can now arouse an uncommon weariness or hostility heightened by the fact that writers only faintly interested in a truthful rendering of Negro life and character have exploited a popular interest.

Exploitation can of course corrupt or even ruin a genuine native force, but nearly every venture in American art and literature has been subjected to its attacks; and since cults are our habit perhaps their extremes can be borne the more easily by hardy Americans. Danger lies as much with the forces of reaction as with those of ecstasy or exploitation. Through the involvements of a secondary argument those natural responses may be diminished or lost by which any art must thrive. If the

American memory were not miraculously short the absorption in Negro art and character would not possess that glitter of newness from which cults are created and from which serious criticism is likely to turn in distaste. This absorption is neither new nor ephemeral; it is in fact a partial culmination of a long stream of expression in which the white American and the Negro have often joined.

Even the Uncle Remus stories and the spirituals collected soon after the Civil War belong to the nearer foreground of time. Records of travels in America of the late eighteenth and early nineteenth century are full of small references to Negro music. Negro rowing-songs rose like barbaric chants along the Ohio and the Mississippi and were remembered by travelers on their way into the farther West. A Western poet declared that Negro songs celebrating the vicissitudes of river navigation and the excitements of the coon hunt were among the earliest original verses of the West. These rudimentary pieces have been lost for the most part: but up and down the country the Negro was soon drawn on the stage in a series of sketches which attempted a close portraiture. These were boldly continued in the early thirties by Jim Crow Rice, who was white. His songs, dances, and lingo followed those of Negroes on the plantations and rivers of the Southwest. A few years later, in 1842, blackface minstrelsy took up the strain.

This improbable medium provides the outlines of a

Negro tradition, broken though it often was by alien elements. Minstrelsy has long been considered a white man's travesty in which the Negro was burlesqued. To the primitive comic sense, to be black is to be funny, and many minstrels made the most of the simple appeal. This exploitation was resented by the anti-slavery leaders of an early period; in the end they went far toward creating the idea that the Negro lacked humor. After the Civil War it would still have been possible to reveal the many-sided Negro of the old plantations, but minstrelsy with its air of irreverence seems to have blocked the way. Because the minstrels had sported with the Negro and had sentimentalized his lot in a few songs, because of his tragic fate and a wish to prove that he possessed moral worth, dignity, and capacity, for the time at least his friends collected and discussed and displayed only his religious pieces. None the less, early minstrelsy offered a rounded portraiture which is only now coming into a genuine completion.

Many minstrels of the forties and fifties had lived in the South and West and knew the Negro at first hand. One of them saw an old peddler of watermelons with a donkey cart in a Georgia town, followed him about until he had mastered his lingo, cries, and snatches of song, as well as his odd manner. The portrayals, so freshly caught, were whole and rich. Emotion welled up in the small acts and through the olios. Tragic implications appeared.

Forrest declared that he knew no finer piece of tragic acting than the impersonation of Dan Bryant as the hungry Negro in *Old Times Rocks,* a minstrel sketch.

The surviving songs and dances of early blackface minstrelsy show Negro origins even though they were often claimed by white composers. Dan Emmett declared that he wrote "Ole Dan Tucker" as a boy of fifteen or sixteen, but this song had a curious history for an independent piece of musical composition. Its air resembles Negro airs; the chorus with its shouting refrain breaks away from the verses in the habitual manner of Negro choruses. And Emmett offered more than one version of the words in which appear those brief and cryptic animal fables that have proved to be a consistent Negro creation—

> Jaybird in de martin's nest,
> To sabe his soul he got no rest.
> Ole Tucker in de foxes' den,
> Out come de young ones nine or ten.
>
> High-hole in de holler tree,
> He poke his bill in for to see,
> De lizard cotch 'im by de snout,
> He call for Tucker to pull 'im out.

In another version of the song a touch of woe is mingled in an odd colloquy.

> Sheep an' hog a-walkin' in de pasture,
> Sheep says, "Hog, can't you go no faster?"
> Hush! Hush! honey, hear de wolf a howlin',
> Ah, ah, de Lawd, de bulldog growlin'.

Most of these fables contained a simple allegory. The crow was a comic symbol for the Negro himself, though he might at times take the form of a sheep or a hog, while the master or the overseer or the patrol—the "patter-roller"—was the bulldog or sometimes the bullfrog. But the note was not always that of fear. In "Clar de Kitchen," one of Rice's popular dance-songs, a fragmentary bird and animal fable appears with triumph for the Negro submerged and disguised:

> A jaybird sot on a hickory limb,
> He winked at me and I winked at him,
> I picked up a stone and I hit his shin,
> Says he, you better not do that agin.
>
> A bullfrog dressed in soger's close
> Went in de field to shoot some crows,
> De crows smell powder an' fly away,
> De bullfrog mighty mad dat day.

In all these fables touches of satire were present, directed toward the white man or toward the Negro himself, when he figured as the lumbering hog or sheep or gave himself wit as a fox or a crow. Self-parody appeared in such dances with bird-calls as "Turkey in de Straw," which Emmett claimed as his own but which surely went back to a Negro dance-song.

Emmett, who belonged to the first minstrel troupe and who became the great song-writer for minstrelsy in its early period, can only have borrowed these songs and dances and fables. "Ole Dan Tucker" underwent those possessive, affectionate changes and additions which mean that many hands have been at work; the melody showed variations; the character was likewise variable. Dan Tucker was pictured as a vagabond, laughed at and scorned by his own kind but constantly bobbing up with outrageous small adventures. Since he consorted with the two sagest creatures of the animal world, the fox and the jaybird, he was endowed with a comical magic: yet he remained the outcast, looming large as he combed his hair with a wagon-wheel, shrinking small and growing ridiculous as he washed his face in a frying-pan, and at last through the transformations of many years changing from black to white.

Emmett's family had been among the early pioneers in Virginia; in later years his father's house in Ohio became a station for the underground railroad. In the middle 1820's he was stationed as a fifer in Kentucky and then at a barracks on the Mississippi below St. Louis. He had traveled through the West with a small circus company in the thirties; and these companies usually included at least one Negro dancer. For a time he played with Rice, who from the first had turned to the Negro for songs and for a direct portraiture. Thus through his impressionable years Emmett was brought into close contact with Negro sources; indeed these possessed his mind.

Some of his songs were close to the spirituals. The opening stanza of his first version of "Dixie" contains a touch of the characteristic Biblical picturing—

Dis worl' was made in jess six days
An' finished up in various ways—
　　Look away! look away! look away! Dixie Land!
Dey den made Dixie trim and nice
But Adam called it Paradise—
　　Look away! look away! look away! Dixie Land!

The verbal phrasing here is unlike that of the Negro, which is swift and elliptical; controversy has in fact gathered around the entire question of the composition of "Dixie," and Emmett has been denied even the smaller glory of transcription. Whatever the circumstance, the Biblical touch is not to be found in other songs of lighter mood in this period; and traces of Negro origin appear in the cries of the chorus and in the melody, which sounds like a fiddler's tune. Elsewhere Emmett often used the Jordan theme. In his "Jordan Is a Hard Road to Trabbel" a fragment of the story of David and Goliath is joined with topical references to make a comic song. In his "Here We Are, or Cross Ober Jordan" the river symbolizes another river of freedom for the Negro, the Ohio.

The climax of the minstrel performance, the walk-around, with its competitive dancing in the mazes of a circle, was patterned after Negro dances in the compounds of the great plantations. Often the walkarounds were composed only of bold pantomime and matched dancing, accompanied by strident cries and the simplest binding of words, which gained color from slave life. Plantation cries, wailing cries, stirring shouts with a tonic

beat ran through all early minstrelsy. With these came
the color of a regional life. "Sugar in de gourd" and
"honey in de horn" were heard in minstrel songs as well
as in southwestern talk. Boatsongs that are clearly related to songs of the flatboatmen of the Ohio and the
Mississippi were highly popular in minstrelsy through
the forties and fifties. Whether or not the tall tale was
characteristic of the Negro or whether he borrowed its
art from the backwoodsman may never be known, since
in an uncharted history the early improvisations have
been lost; but the magnification that belonged to the
story-telling of the Southwest appeared in occasional minstrel songs, usually with a twist that differentiated them
from the frontier tales, like that which described the
fabulous little black bull, Hoosen Johnny—

> He shake his tail, he jar de ribber,
> Hoosen Johnny, Hoosen Johnny,
> He shake his tail, he jar de ribber,
> Long time ago.

Further coloring was given by Irish reels, jigs, and lilts;
the Negro seemed to pick up the Irish musical idiom with
facility from Irish immigrants in the West. One of Emmett's Jordan songs moves to an Irish lilt, yet it keeps a
Biblical picturing in the fashion of the spirituals.

Early blackface minstrelsy revealed indeed the natural
appropriations of the Negro from the life about him: but
the persistent stress was primitive, the effect exotic and

strange with the swaying figures and black faces of the minstrels lighted by guttering gas flames or candlelight on small country stages or even in the larger theaters. Within this large and various pattern lay a fresh context of comedy, plain in the intricate, grotesque dancing as the minstrels "walked jaw-bone" or accomplished the deep complications of the "dubble trubble" or the "grapevine twist." A bold comic quality appeared which had not developed elsewhere in American humor, that of nonsense. With all his comic wild excesses the backwoodsman never overflowed into pure nonsense; the Yankee did not display it. Perhaps the Negro did not invent the nonsensical narratives told in song on the minstrel stage, but the touch is akin to that of Negro fables in song; and nonsense in minstrelsy shows a sharp distinction from other humor of the day.

> A little old man was ridin' by,
> His horse was tryin' to kick a fly,
> He lifted his leg towards de south
> An' sent it bang in its own mouth—
>
> An' sich a-gittin' upstairs
> An' a-playin' on de fiddle,
> Sich a-gittin' upstairs I nebber did see,
> Sich a-gittin' upstairs an' a-playin' on de fiddle,
> Sich a-gittin' upstairs I nebber did see.

The note of triumph, dominant in all early American humor, appeared in these reflected creations of the Negro, but not as triumph over circumstance. Rather this was an unreasonable headlong triumph launching into the realm of the preposterous. It could be heard in the careless phrasing of the songs, in the swift pulsations of their rhythms. Yet defeat was also clear. Slavery was constantly imaged in brief phrases or in simple situations. Fragments of cryptic work-songs were heard—

Sheep shell oats, ole Tucker shell de corn.

Echoes sounded of the forbidden devil songs—

Oh, I'se sorry I sold myself to the debbil.

Defeat was hinted in the occasional minor key and in the smothered sidelong satire. In American humor the sudden extreme of nonsense was new, and the tragic undertone was new.

Primitive elements survived in blackface minstrelsy long after its outlines had been stylized in the seventies and eighties, and the minstrel show had become a medley of Irish and German songs and even of Jewish impersonations. Something of ritual was kept in the patter of interlocutor and endmen and in the emotional resurgences of the choruses and the dancing. But it is a mistake to consider that only the Negro has offered primitive elements in American expression. During the years in which his songs and fables and dances were coming into recognition a widespread comic lore amounting to a folklore, striated with primitive elements, was gathering about the Yankee, the backwoodsman, and a few lesser native types. The really striking circumstance is that the Negro through the medium of minstrelsy occupied an all but equal place with these figures. In the thirties Jim Crow Rice gained a popularity said to be exceeded by that of no other comedian of his time. The appeal of Negro songs was insistent and enduring. "The Ethiopian melodies well deserve to be called, as they are in fact, the national airs of America," wrote Bayard Taylor in 1849. "They follow the American race in all its migrations, colonizations, and conquests." Taylor was writing from California, where minstrelsy was heard almost as soon as the first gold-seeker set foot there. A minstrel song, Foster's "O Susannah!" became a rallying-cry for the new empire, a song of meeting and parting made into nonsense, a fiddler's tune with a Negro beat and a touch of smothered pathos in the melody. Foster had often turned to Negro camp-meetings for melodies; and all his songs were promptly adopted by the minstrels.

No doubt part of the appeal of minstrelsy came from its draughts upon a common reminiscence, since many aspects of the pioneer experience were crystallized there. Part of its popularity surely arose from the fact that a strong primitive underply was spread through the life of the country in those formative years; the expression of the Negro created a natural response. Minstrelsy even stirred a considerable bulk of esthetic speculation. Tilts took place between genteel critics and a few lawless spirits who saw in the minstrel songs a new and original art. The songs were welcomed abroad. Whitman found in the Negro dialect hints of "a modification of all the words of the English language, for musical purposes, for a native grand opera in America." Indeed in the fifties more than one prediction of blackface grand opera was formulated. A little later, with the strong continuance of minstrelsy, came a query echoed by makers of the cult of the Negro in the present day, "Is the Caucasian played out?" A renewed wave of absorption appeared after the Civil War and lasted through the seventies and eighties, with the vogue of the Uncle Remus stories and the recapture of a few other Negro legends centering about the same figure, but more savage and grotesque in character than those assembled by Harris.

Traditions for a Negro literature are thoroughly grounded, existing for the most part in fragmentary songs and brief tales, but as a literature none the less. A vast amount of critical work remains to be done in disentangling elements unmistakably of Negro origin in minstrel songs from those created by the white composer or adapter. Songs obviously belonging to the Negro remain uncollected except as these appear occasionally in general anthologies. For the most part they can be discovered only in the fascinating morasses of collections of sheet music. On the whole the Negro tradition has been no more unfortunate than many other popular American strains; a great bulk of our native lore has been lost, and much is still to be recovered. With the full assembling of the Negro tradition a gauge might be provided against false exploitation, and the finer productions of the present day might take on unexaggerated values. Regarded as the outcome of a slowly established lore, a swift or sudden development would not be expected either from the Negro or from those white artists preoccupied with Negro themes who have had so many homely predecessors. It might be easier to remember that the progress of all literatures has been that of a gradual enrichment.

American Art: A Possible Future

IN NONE of the arts has our full native inheritance been clarified. It has been our fortune to create briefly, hastily, insecurely, and then to press on to some new and not always clearly understood objective, with the result that the arts in this country have shown many brave beginnings and few developments, and even these have often been casually buried and are to be found now only by excavation, like the artifacts of a forgotten city.

These careless approaches may prove to have been excellent for a people whose intentions are still experimental and who, presumably, have been trying to create arts distinctively their own. Much has been made of our "cultural lag," our lack of consistent esthetic purposes. But it is doubtful whether the beginnings of any art are ever orderly, and when patterns have become sharply grooved they are usually lifeless. Our so-called "lag" may be nothing of the kind. Instead we may be moving with hesitation in new directions.

Within the last dozen years one of our periodic rushes of rediscovery of our past has occurred; and if the evaluations are conflicting, gradually many hidden facts have been coming to the surface. In music a whole continuous underply begins to emerge, pre-Handelian, based primarily upon the dance, continued in part by the religious songs of the early New England singing schools, by both white and Negro spirituals, and by the British ballads, spreading into fiddle-tunes and songs of the southern mountains and of the range and lumber-camp, often mixed with other musical materials and showing original variations on new soil and under new conditions, and consistently maintained even to the present day in widely scattered areas. Here indeed is a whole musical heritage, affording something more than folk-tunes for musical decoration, rather to be used as European composers of the past have used a similar but not identical music, for a fundamental native schooling.

For years critics have lamented the absence of an American folklore and, building from this hypothesis, have formed dreary conclusions as to the future of the American arts. But our folklore is now seen to be abundant. Enough of this has come to the surface to indicate that, whatever its derivations, it is unlike that of other peoples in its essential patterns. Through it our early fantasies and mythologies are coming back to us, showing the secure beginnings of a native poetry and a native language; and the flow of these patterns into literary expression can be traced from Hawthorne and Melville to Mark Twain and Emily Dickinson and Edwin Arlington Robinson.

Our painting seems to have behind it less consistent

traditions than our music and literature, but it would be well not to dogmatize about this in view of unpredictable discoveries in the other arts. And interpretations have often been wide of the mark. A favorite argument has been that the Puritan builder suppressed ornament as the result of a deliberate process of theological reasoning and that the blight has spread among us down the years. But, though the average Puritan had considerable power as a dialectician, it seems doubtful whether with hammer and saw in hand he often exercised this power and blocked an earthy impulse. For one thing, those using hammer and saw in the seventeenth and eighteenth centuries were not likely to be Puritans. The proportion of yeomen and journeymen was very large who remained outside the fold of the theocracy, even though it was to their clear advantage to enter.

Puritan and non-Puritan alike were influenced in this long period by the tendency toward the abstract in Calvinistic theology, and equally by the general turn toward abstraction which came in England with the Reformation and took many speculative forms. Puritan or non-Puritan, the journeyman builder belonged pretty much to his time. Instead of his being thwarted, it seems likely that abstract values gave him an undefined pleasure, that he even took a sensuous delight in the elimination of ornamental detail. Certainly form, strict but apparently casual, was rarely lacking in what he created. Its quality may be traced in everything to which he and his race have turned their minds, from meeting houses and clipper ships to metaphor and idiom. And this circumstance can be pressed toward the conclusion that the New Englander, with his self-contained creative powers and his passion for migration, left his distinctive print wherever he went in this country, creating a tendency among us toward the abstract which has been strong if unconscious and not as yet fully developed.

As for the pioneer of all ancestries or regional affiliations, a familiar theory has it that he was destructive of the amenities and the arts, but like many other generalizations about American life and the American character this does not bear the test of a close scrutiny of the record. Women often carried portraits or clocks with glass paintings or delicate china on their laps in oxcarts over hundreds of miles into the Western wilderness, and their children often kept these intact. In a Tennessee cabin I have seen a silver luster cup of exquisite shape, which had been broken into small fragments and coarsely mended, but which had been preserved with pride and pleasure for its esthetic values and its symbol of a tradition; and similar evidences will be found on almost every one of our successive frontiers.

Perhaps too much has been made of the folk-handicrafts, the carvings, whittlings, wrought iron, flower paintings, hooked rugs, woven bedspreads, and homespun, of the pioneer. These often have lasting creative values and join with other evidences to suggest the basis for a native

approach; but what becomes more important in retrospect is the recurrent proof that they afford of visual and
tactile skills and the steady, widespread use of these. Pioneer experience was extraordinarily full of subtle preoccupations for the eye and hand. To follow a hardly discernible path or trace in the forests, to notice slight essential
changes in vegetation, in falling light, in contours of the
ground, in the undercurrents of watercourses, was part
of a necessary habit which extended through several
American generations and is still to be found among many
whose break with the land seems almost complete. And
the typical pioneer or frontiersman was master of those
daily and primitive arts that have often afforded an ancestry for the fine arts. His supple handling of weapons,
his use of skins and furs, his construction of necessary
tools, and not least his free sense of personal decoration,
were all firmly restricted by economy of use and means
and indicate in outline the esthetic approach.

As for an outcome in larger forms of expression, did this
exist? We are impatient for an outcome; we always have
been. From an early day, almost from the close of the
Revolution and possibly before, our expectations as to esthetic fulfillment have been nothing short of stupendous.
All at once we were to have all the arts, on the epical
scale. Small Western newspapers foretold the certain event
in the eighteen thirties and forties. We are still strangely
afflicted by that obsession. Because the grandiose fulfillment has been lacking we have failed to perceive small

but hardy evidences of those fresh forms and fresh approaches which would seem the natural result of an era of discovery, and may form beginnings for distinctive arts.

Woodcuts revealing new native types of the frontier and the backwoods with a sure linear attack and a pungent humor may be found scattered in old almanacs. As one turns old engravings on some single subject, say that of the Indian, here and there a striking bit of composition will appear, with primitive qualities boldly transcribed in terms of light and arrangement. Often these effects will be incomplete, shown only in a single passage of a drawing, set against a trite, blurred notion of what the wilderness was like. These evidences are likely to be highly discontinuous. The name attached to an interesting piece may not easily be found again. Many are unsigned. To draw together those of genuine worth over a period of years would mean a long search through humble sources, and because of our odd bias away from the popular arts (odd in a democracy) they are often difficult to find. The casual fate that has overtaken Audubon's drawings, so sure and so original in color and design, is an indication of our established tendency to overlook any but the formal evidences of an art. And it is only recently, through the discoveries and interpretations of such critics as Mr. Holger Cahill and the Nadelmans, that American folk-painting and sculpture—"the art of the common man"—has received any recognition whatever.

Even in their own day this expression was probably

brief and fragmentary. Experiment was continually being blotted out, not by the scornful and destructive pioneer but by forces beyond his control. Whatever was created, whatever took shape out of a formative culture, was likely to be destroyed by the mere force of migration, acting like a vast physical upheaval, destroying small, tangible things and always tending to eliminate them, whatever the wish of women in oxcarts with their clocks and their delicate china. The related destructive force was that of fire. Native beginnings, particularly in the visual arts because of their destructible character, were reduced by repeated holocausts which extended from the burning of cabins and stockades in New England, as the result of Indian raids, down to the mid-century bonfires of cloth-and-paper-towns in California, and onward to the action of Mrs. O'Leary's cow, and indeed to a very recent day. Fire in this country has been a large and obvious yet unreckoned anti-cultural agency, and must be counted as part of the cost of making new, rash, primitive beginnings. For the rather hazy, popular theory as to the destructive nature of the pioneer, another, simpler reading of the record can be substituted.

2

Naturally European esthetics and the European arts have been an influence upon all our creative expression;

but in literature and music the invasion seems to have been more gradual than in painting, and perhaps more easily assimilated. For the visual arts the first great influx apparently began with the Crystal Palace Exhibition in London in 1851, when under the sway of Albert, the lush Victorian abundance began to burgeon and bloom with a vengeance. Immediately we had in New York our own feebler Crystal Palace, and a gaudy, insipid acreage of oils so quickly became the rage that the auction rooms of the infant town of San Francisco were filled with them, advertised as specially imported from abroad. What Lewis Mumford has called a "pillage of the past" followed so quickly and feverishly that the possibility of assimilation was excluded, and the drive from the American center was continued by the pull of the foreign schools.

In the practical arts, on the other hand, it was readily taken for granted in this country that native skills could be developed on native ground, and they were, as in the unique and cunning designs of clipper ships and in the widening number of mechanical inventions. But as to the fine arts a false notion was dominant, a notion that by no means was peculiarly American. The artificial division between the practical and the fine arts had long since taken place in Europe, with the result that the one tended to be lost or obscured and the other separated from vigorous and natural sources.

Let us lay this burden for a moment at the already over-crowded door of the *bourgeoisie*. The natural interpenetration of the fine and the practical arts had been broken by the recession of the guilds and the rise of the small capitalist class. An instinctive functioning had been left behind. A whole outcome cannot of course be given any single ascription, and the tendency of the Reformation (or the turn of thought that was most highly concentrated in the Reformation) had likewise a disruptive and divisive effect as abstract and intellectual elements were introduced into the concrete cultures of Europe.

In other words, American painting began to take shape in the midst of a thorough and widespread confusion of aims, and for us confusion has been worse confounded because a difficult cultural destiny has been upon us from the beginning. On the whole, the European groups among us have meant to cast Europe behind them; yet a persistent awareness of Europe, of European values, of what Europe has thought of us and what we have thought of Europeans has been steadily with us. This awareness has become the sharper because Europeans have bent themselves to the task of judging our attainments with thoroughness in a great amount of letterpress.

We have both fought these judgments and yielded to them. Our mixed attitudes—our languishing wish to conform to European standards and our sensitive belligerence —appear strongly even in the folk-plays of our early stage. They recur in the explosive, highly posed, toplofty humor of *Innocents Abroad* and *A Connecticut Yankee at King Arthur's Court*. Our relation to Europe is a subject which we have never been able to let alone. We have been obsessed by it, and we haven't known what to do about it.

In the visual arts and in art criticism the dilemma has been particularly acute. The more or less explicit idea governing most of our art criticism has been that our art would naturally become a sequence within the art of western Europe. With enough European schooling and a sufficiently large number of civilized contacts, it has been hoped that esthetically we might at last begin to develop. We had only to catch up with Europe, so to speak, by diligent study.

This is to disregard the ways in which cultures have grown and been sustained in the past. Most cultures have at some time been subject to foreign influences, but surely the center of growth of any distinctive culture is to be found within the social organism and is created by peculiar and irreducible social forces. It is plain, as Franz Boas says in his introduction to Ruth Benedict's recent *Patterns of Culture,* that "hardly any trait of culture can be understood taken out of its general setting." And Dr. Benedict insists as her major thesis upon "the importance of the study of the whole configuration as over against the continued analysis of its parts."

Dr. Benedict cites Worringer as showing "how fundamental a difference this approach makes in the field of esthetics," and Worringer's argument has its suggestion for ourselves. "He contrasts the highly developed art of two periods, the Greek and the Byzantine. The older criticism, he insists, which defined art in absolute terms and identified it with classical standards, could not possibly understand the processes of art as they are represented in Byzantine painting or mosaic. Achievement in one cannot be judged in terms of the other, because each was attempting to achieve quite different ends. The Greeks in their art attempted to give expression to their own pleasure in activity; they sought to embody an identification of their vitality with the objective world. Byzantine art, on the other hand, objectified abstraction, a profound feeling of separation in the face of outside nature. Any understanding of the two must take account, not only of comparisons of artistic ability, but far more of differences of artistic intention. The two were contrasting, integrated configurations, each of which could make use of forms and standards that were incredible to the other."

Now whether or not so positive a contrast exists between our artistic intention and that of European groups, the fact remains that our "configuration" is not the European "configuration," either socially or geographically. And whether or not we derived our early motivating ideas from Europe, these have been shaped to our own distinctive ends. It would seem obvious that our art, if we are to have one, must spring from the center rather than from the periphery of our social pattern. Yet our criticism on the whole has considered European art in the absolute terms to which Worringer refers, and has related American art to this as if no basic differences existed between the groups of civilizations. Oriental influences have been discussed as though it were a mere matter of individual cleverness to assimilate them. To follow a single phase of Worringer's argument, a general attitude toward nature may prevail among us (and probably does) which is wholly different from that which prevails in England or in Spain, and this should lead to differences in expression; yet certain artistic achievements in England or in Spain are considered as absolutes which we should imitate. The results of such experiments will necessarily be faltering.

Our painting has never been fully considered in its native cultural relations and implications or basic intentions, nor is this strange, since the elements of our culture are only now being discovered and defined, and indeed the whole movement toward such explicit cultural definitions anywhere is comparatively a new one.

3

A fumbling effort to create an indigenous art appeared early in stress upon the American subject. The spectacular Indian was brought to the fore, and painting on this theme was largely bad because we never in any sense assimilated the Indian, and because Americans of an early period were governed by two extreme ideas, that Indians were savages who must be exterminated, and that they were figures in a primitive idyll.

This last, deriving from Rousseau, still obtains among many Americans who are creatively adrift, and may persist because certain tribal cultures, particularly that of the Pueblos of New Mexico, present definition and completion while ours is chaotic. Dr. Benedict might go further and suggest that what she calls the balanced Apollonian culture of the Pueblos offers a resting place for imperfect Dionysians like ourselves. Undoubtedly there is a good deal of wear and tear in being Dionysian, and our efforts in that direction have sometimes been particularly strenuous. But whether this small group of Apollonians—the Pueblos—can offer us a point of artistic departure is another matter. We should be obliged to go the whole way with Mary Austin as to the fundamental American rhythm, and then find a reason for selecting this one, highly distinctive tribe as a prototype for ourselves.

Consciousness of the American subject continued intermittently through the nineteenth century, in the abundant production of the Hudson River School, in those great mossy, green and brown dioramic landscapes that seem inspired by the American poems of Felicia Hemans but that do somehow convey something characteristic of the American scene. The paintings of Inness reveal that "proprietary sense" of our landscape which Mr. Gutheim has noted. But though that geographic adaptation and expression which Mr. Gutheim has outlined appeared in all the arts, there were plenty of divergences. Church, Hunt, Washington Allston, LaFarge, both the Giffords, Martin,

Whistler, used alien or remotely symbolical subjects, sometimes to the exclusion of others, and the emphasis soon began to shift to techniques.

At the turn of the century came the overwhelming discovery that subject was unimportant. The American subject was tacitly, sometimes openly derided; it was certainly left behind by American art students in the foreign schools as they began to thread the mazes of highly intellectualized modern theory and experiment. The powerful innovations of post-impressionism, *surréalisme,* and the rest became magnets. Now by another whirl we seem to have returned to the American subject as primary. This emphasis may have been dictated by recent necessity, but a school of renewed conviction has apparently arisen as part of the general move toward—or back to—a sometimes militant regionalism.

The apparently simple approach for the American artist by way of the American subject can offer plenty of pitfalls. The painting of Grant Wood, with its American types and regional backgrounds and themes, has all the orthodox elements of a native art, but this painter many times used superficial and transient elements of the American subject without touching its core. To make paintings look like crewel work, presumably because crewels were a familiar American medium (usually a bad one) is a regression quite as definite as would be another orgy of burnt wood, undertaken because the poker and the oak plank were easy to come by in the American home

before the passing of the stove. To give a portrait in oils
the style of a daguerreotype even to the shine of the cop-
per base, presumably because the daguerreotype has
played a large part among us, is an extreme sentimentalism that has nothing to do with the art of painting. Grant
Wood seems at his best in some of his more casual decorations where a conscious purpose has less play, or in direct
satire, for which a solid native tradition exists in the precise field which he has chosen, the portraiture of the type
—a tradition which has established itself through many
forms of our folk humor.

Yet a wide use of the environmental subject would seem
peculiarly necessary for us because of our situation as a
people whose culture is still undefined and incomplete.
We do not know our land as peoples of older, smaller
countries know theirs. Because of our continual mobility
we lack a deeply rooted and instinctive knowledge of the
underlying natural forms by which we are surrounded.
We have rarely submitted for long to the discipline of
place, though in the large we have been shaped by its
earthy elements. Turner, Huntington, Ellen Semple and
others have analyzed the power of the land in the forma-
tion of our societies, and its force appears outside social
economies. Rhythms of hill and bottom land and prairie
and mountain, native qualities of light or murk, have left
their print upon the social mind and imagination. They
have been—they still are—among our esthetic and cultural
determinants.

It is not that we require mere faithful transcriptions of our sharply varied landscape or shore, or of the peculiar, stratified aggregations which make the American city, though these might offer more to a people still in process of self-recognition than the exponents of "pure" art would be willing to admit. Socially considered, there would seem to be a wide place for the honest journeyman painter—for the honest and simple pleasures of recognition. Beyond this, the land remains formative in a strict esthetic sense. Outer subject—the mere American scene—may fall away. Many artists may soon leave this behind, but the inalienable patterns will remain.

In the same way the American type and its many variations may become something more than visual material. Posture, gesture, movement, bone structure, ranges of individual expression—these inevitably suggest underlying social ideas and emotions and motives in terms of typical form. They provide clues to the governing complexes which belong to us and which make our culture distinctive from that of others.

Those who have derided subject are in a sense right. Our eager young art students who have been swept away by every new theory have their justification. They have sought a perception by means of which the final transcendence of art over its materials may be accomplished. It is obvious that in any final expression subject becomes secondary. Their mistake has been to suppose that such perceptions can be discovered in a vacuum anywhere.

They have failed to notice that the young foreign artists with whom they have associated have all had an initial, unconscious schooling which the American lacks. The young foreign artist has of course long traditions in the arts which may be used in sequence or for departure: but even more significantly, he knows his environment and his native culture through association with others who look upon the outer world with eyes not unlike his own, and who suggest identities by a thousand communicative means—idiom, intonation, gesture, dress, social choices. Whatever his individual variation, he can draw unconsciously from a whole flux of basic social patterns. With us such patterns are not yet abundantly established, or are still unrecognized.

4

Let us lay down the principle that the American artist cannot take off from the same points of departure as the European artist. Let us accept the fact that it is futile for the American artist to try to "catch up" with Europeans because at best he is trying, often obscurely, to do something of his own.

In his complicated but really rather thrilling dilemma, the environmental subject will be one clue to native forms —an elementary discipline. His further and more difficult problem is to draw upon the many subtle evidences of an unfolding tradition. A process of discovery and rediscovery is going on, just now with acceleration, but until the materials of all our culture become known and are easily possessed the creative worker in any of the arts will necessarily be thwarted.

Here and there indications appear as to the stimulus and reinforcement which these materials may give to the painter. Our still half-buried folklore abounds in the purely legendary, and in this, essential American types, rather than characters, have been drawn and redrawn. Basic traceries are there which might be full of suggestion to the mural painter. This is not at all to propose that he should apotheosize Mike Fink and Davy Crockett, John Henry and Paul Bunyan, though these legendary heroes might lend themselves well to mural treatment. But the strong, prevailing legendary quality, with its native biases, naturally would have much to say to him, because the sense of legend lies broadly at the base of mural painting. From this special abundance he could gain a quite positive sense of direction.

As one reads consistent signs in our cultural history it would seem that very great sequences of mural painting should develop among us. This is a highly social art, and we have always gathered easily in crowds. A dozen reasons—timidity among them—might be mentioned as to why we have left empty the walls of our many gathering-places. An acute sense of the more conspicuous phases of social expression among us, as in revivals, camp-meetings, political demonstrations, lodges, parades, and even

lynching, might give the American muralist a knowledge
of basic social outlines as well as an extended range of
materials. Thomas Benton has used some of these. A wide
understanding of the dominating social forces might reveal subjects of quite a different order from those which
he has chosen. And if our painters were fortunate enough
to know well some of the folk-satire directed against our
early flamboyant oratory, it may be that the lack of control, the tendency toward excess, which often afflicts our
artists when they approach large subjects or utilize large
spaces, would be objectified and reduced.

The American painter might gain assurance in a contemporary mode if he knew by heart the spare abstract as
this appears in many phases of our folk-expression, particularly within the New England tradition. Woven into all
our folklore is an acute observation of the external world
which any artist could afford to know well, and this tends
to be poetic rather than naturalistic. It is typically in key
with the abstract. Indeed a full knowledge of our folklore
and folk-song would reveal the subordinate place that
naturalism constantly took in our early free expression.
This absence in itself may constitute a tradition, and the
underlying poetry and humor might give the artist something of the lift which he must have if subject and technique are not to leave him in chains.

This is by no means to lay down the thesis that the
painter must be schooled in all the arts. The talent of
many painters seems to be channeled in the single mode.

But in the large, the problem for the American artist is a cultural problem, and it is only through a full appropriation of our cultural tendencies that the sound frame of native reference, which major painting requires, can be provided.

If such appropriations cannot easily become an individual matter, it is true that certain artists have accomplished them. In our own time Marin has overpassed the demands of subject and has used that turn toward purity of color and abstraction, which have a secure place in our traditions, with a humorous assertion of personal idiosyncrasy which anyone familiar with forms of our character will immediately recognize. I know that Burchfield has been regarded as an unsparing realist and even as a satirist, but it seems to me that what he accomplishes is not an exposure of facts but a synthesis of certain deeplying qualities in American life. He is acutely aware of its melodrama, which has often appeared with a kind of driving poetry, infusing ugly materials. If, as has been said, his deserted mansions stand aloof from the earth on which they are planted, this separation from environment has been a large part of our experience.

The individual artist must always make his own special discoveries, but we shall gain if he is not pressed too hard to attain them, if he need not make them alone. The greater ones will survive the effort, but wastage and bewilderment will continue among lesser men who are too good to lose. A sensitive historical criticism would seem a major necessity, broadly grounded in native research as well as in esthetics. A prodigious amount of work is still to be done in the way of unearthing, defining, and synthesizing our traditions, and finally in making them known through simple and natural means. Beneath this purpose must probably lie fresh reconstructions of our notion as to what constitutes a culture, with a removal of ancient snobberies and with new inclusions.

This is not in any conceivable sense to advocate a policy of artistic isolation. With all the support that definitions of our own traditions may give him, the American artist will necessarily run full-on sooner or later into the uncertainties and over-pliant ambitions which now seem to cut across all expression everywhere. He cannot escape his fate all at once, as an American with a partially illegible and syncopated history behind him, or as a citizen of a world that now seems to face many economic, social, and cultural crossroads. Yet recognition of the peculiar elements which form American culture would seem fundamental for both the artist and the critic, whether or not they wholly like what they find.

The intellectualized self-consciousness which was a partial outcome of the Reformation and which has developed through the intervening centuries is apparently besetting all artists everywhere. With all his handicaps the American artist has at least the advantage of a fairly complete background for this mode. It began for us with the landing of the Pilgrims and was continued by fine-spun arguments in all the theologies. The intellectualized, self-conscious attack has become in a general way a national habit, even a rough technique. This technique can be turned toward the definition and solution of our difficult cultural problems. Perhaps the American artist cannot now assume those simple and intuitive attitudes which the artist always wants—which most of us want—but he may consciously work toward a discovery of our traditions, attempt to use them, and eventually take his inevitable place.

Index

297